REPORT CARD ON

Report Cards

ALTERNATIVES TO CONSIDER

EDITED BY

TARA AZWELL AND
ELIZABETH SCHMAR

HEINEMANN

PORTSMOUTH, NH

This book is dedicated to our colleagues, and our students and their parents, who have helped us expand our picture of what school can be.

Heinemann
A division of Reed Elsevier Inc.
361 Hanover Street
Portsmouth, NH 03801–3912

Offices and agents throughout the world

We would like to thank those who have given their permission to include material in this book. Every effort has been made to contact the copyright holders for permission to reprint borrowed material where necessary. We regret any oversights that may have occurred and would be happy to rectify them in future printings of this work.

Figure 9–2 from *Practical Aspects of Authentic Assessment: Putting the Pieces Together* by Bonnie Campbell–Hill and Cynthia Ruptic. Copyright © 1994 by Christopher–Gordon Publishers, Inc. Reprinted by permission.

Library of Congress Cataloging-in-Publication Data

Report card on report cards / edited by Tara Azwell, Elizabeth Schmar.
     p. cm.
   Includes bibliographical references.
   ISBN 0-435-08842-4
   1. Grading and marking (Students)—United States.   2. Educational evaluation—United States.   I. Azwell, Tara S.   II. Schmar, Elizabeth.
   LB3051.R365   1995
   371.2'72—dc20   94-45704
                                                         CIP

Editor: Carolyn Coman
Cover design: Catherine Hawkes

Printed in the United States of America on acid-free paper
98 97 96 95   EB   1 2 3 4 5 6

Contents

About the Authors

TARA AZWELL

A twenty-year elementary classroom teacher who is currently an associate professor of reading and language arts in the Teachers College, Emporia State University. She has served as president of the Kansas Reading Association, president of Kansas-Teachers Applying Whole Language, and is president-elect of Kansas Reading Professionals in Higher Education. She coauthored *Cooperative Learning in the Elementary School* with Harvey Foyle and Larry Lyman. She served as guest editor of the KASCD *Record* whole language themed issue.

ELIZABETH SCHMAR

A ten-year classroom teacher. Publications include articles in KASCD *Record's* whole language themed issue, *The Whole Language Catalog,* and *Classroom Management and Discipline: A K–12 Guide.* She has served as vice president of Kansas-TAWL and on her school district's assessment and curriculum committees.

TES MEHRING

Associate dean of the Teachers College, Emporia State University. In this capacity, she coordinates graduate and undergraduate programs, supervises the Professional Development School, and teaches graduate and undergraduate courses in psychology, special education, and teacher education. She has received several federal, state, and private foundation grants, and has published a curriculum-based written language test, numerous chapters and several refereed journal articles.

EILEEN HOGAN

Chair of the Division of Early Childhood Education, Emporia State University. She has worked in higher education for twenty years preparing teachers of young children. She writes in the area of multicultural education.

GLENNIE BUCKLEY

Curriculum and instructional specialist for the Topeka, Kansas, public schools. Her administrative responsibilities include K–12 language arts, K–12 remedial reading, K–12 English as a Second Language (ESL), and K–5 Chapter 1. She writes about the role of the central office administrator in the context of site-based decision making. She worked closely with district teachers on the new progress report for Topeka Public Schools. She has taught at the elementary-, middle-school, and high-school levels, and Chapter l and remedial reading classes.

JANE ANDERSON

An elementary and learning disabilities teacher for twenty-three years. She is beginning her eighth year as an elementary principal. She specializes in staff development.

MARCETA REILLY

A preschool and elementary classroom teacher, an elementary building principal, and an assistant superintendent of schools, for twenty-eight years. Currently, she is serving as the superintendent of schools. She has published in the area of parents as volunteers in schools. She facilitates curriculum groups working to develop outcomes, standards, and performance assessment measures.

BARBARA MAUGHMER

An eighteen-year classroom teacher who is currently serving part time as a clinical instructor for Kansas State University's Professional Development Project while teaching first grade half days. She is an active whole language teacher who founded both Manhattan TAWL and Kansas-TAWL. She is currently serving on the board of the Whole Language Umbrella. Publications include articles in the KASCD *Record* whole language themed issue, and NEA's *Student Portfolios.*

BILLIE MANDERICK

A first-grade teacher for seventeen years. She has been recognized as an Outstanding Writing Teacher, Topeka Teacher of the Year, and was nominated for Kansas Teacher of the Year. She has published in the KASCD *Record* whole language themed issue. She has served on numerous district curriculum committees in the areas of language arts, math, and health. She was a member of the district committee to design a new progress report.

DEBBIE TOFFLEMIRE

An elementary classroom teacher who has served on her district's language arts curriculum committee. She is an in-service trainer for the Six-Trait Writing Assessment.

KATHY EGAWA

A classroom teacher who is completing her doctoral work at Indiana University. She has contributed to Harste, Short, and Burke's *Creating Classrooms for Authors and Inquirers* (1995; Portsmouth, NH: Heinemann) and has written in the area of evaluating literacy and collaborating with parents.

KIM YOUNG

A ten-year elementary classroom teacher who is currently serving as an education program consultant for communications for the Kansas State Board of Education. She is past-president of her local reading council and served on her district's language arts committee. She is a frequent presenter at state and national conferences.

LISA BIETAU

A fourteen-year classroom teacher who serves on both local and national curriculum development committees. She has received several grants for work in science and math education. She is a frequent presenter at state and national conferences. She has contributed to the KASCD *Record* whole language themed issue and NRA's *Student Portfolios.*

RICHARD DRIVER

An experienced middle- and high-school math teacher who is presently a curriculum and instructional specialist for the Topeka Public Schools and an adjunct associate professor at Washburn University, teaching statistics and other math courses.

KATHY SCHLOTTERBECK

A twenty-eight-year classroom teacher who has taught hearing-impaired children as well as kindergarten and second- and third-grade children. She is a member of the advisory committee for Kansas-TAWL. She has attended summer institutes in writing workshop and reading workshop with Jane Hansen. She contributed an article to the KASCD *Record* whole language themed issue and is a regular presenter at state conferences.

SANDY ADAMS

A twenty-five-year educator who has served as a building administrator for the past sixteen years. She has been a leader in developing nongraded progress reports in her district.

MIKE KASNIC

Director of Butcher Children's School, Emporia State University. He has written extensively in the area of mathematics education, technology in the school, and curriculum development. He has presented at state and national conferences.

GORDON GULSETH

Primary School Head of The Prairie School in Racine, Wisconsin. He is former chair of the Interest Action Group on Leadership in Whole Language for the Whole Language Umbrella and a founder of Kansas–TAWL. Active in numerous professional organizations, he has presented at state and national conferences. He has served as an elementary school building administrator in Kansas, Colorado, and Wisconsin.

Preface

TARA'S THOUGHTS

In working with teachers and administrators around the state of Kansas, I have come to feel their concern for their students, their schools, and themselves. I have listened to them struggle with the many forces pulling them in different directions. I have experienced their dismay that new programs have been added to their curriculum while nothing has been taken away. I have seen them wrestle with ways to bring their newly developed belief system, instructional strategies, and assessment strategies into congruence while meeting district and state mandates. I have heard their concern that students are being overlooked in our efforts at school improvement. As always, I have heard their despair at having to choose between their commitment to their students and their commitment to themselves and their families when, regardless of how much they have to do, they still only have twenty-four hours in which to do it. Because I myself am dealing with all of the same issues in working with students in my graduate and undergraduate classes, I share their concern.

However, being the eternal optimist that I am (my family regularly accuses me of refusing to live in the world as it is, preferring my own version of the world as it could be), I see some of the current movements for change in our schools as possibilities for examining all of our current practices. We have the opportunity to retain those practices that contribute to the learning of all students, and to reexamine and redesign those practices that are interfering with student learning. We can unload some of the baggage we have brought with us from past paradigms of school.

My hope for this book is that it provides support to teachers and school administrators who are examining their evaluation and reporting systems by providing models of possible ways to accomplish the task. I also hope to raise some questions that may have been unasked by teachers and administrators. My college students are used to my questions about standard classroom practices: "Why are we doing what we are doing? Is it helping or hurting our goal for every child to be a successful learner?" I hope that this book will encourage teachers and school administrators to use the lens of these two questions to examine the reporting systems in place in their schools.

BETH'S THOUGHTS

My search for answers—and a strong sense of frustration—motivated me to work on this book. My first frustration came as a teacher in my own classroom. My teaching methods and assessment techniques did not match my district's traditional report card. Here I was, gathering all of this wonderful and valuable information about my students, yet I had no formal way to share my insights with either parents or students. So I worked with other teachers to develop a more appropriate report form, as we continued using the district form. In essence, we were doing double duty. Using both report forms forced us to gather two kinds of information. The traditional report card required percentages and letter grades with little room for comments. The progress report required observations, performance, and conference, and it contained large spaces for comments. Gathering information and completing two reports for each student became a nightmare!

My second frustration stemmed from a personal experience. After divorcing several years ago, my mother remarried. She and her husband adopted two children, a boy and a girl. So at the age of thirty-one, I had a nine-year-old brother. While I was teaching third grade, my brother was in third grade in a different city. Shawn had some difficulties in math that required the assistance of a paraprofessional daily for his math assignments. Yet, on his report card, Shawn consistently received an S or S+ in math. My mother called me with questions and concerns about whether the grades were a true reflection of ability. As a teacher, I now had the opportunity to give advice to my mother. Unfortunately, I found my answers to her concerns inadequate, and I actually raised more questions for myself than I answered for her. Again, more frustration.

Report Card on Report Cards is written by a collection of diverse people who may not have all of the answers but have shared some of the same frustrations. In this volume, we are sharing with you some of the ways we have found to address our concerns. All of the authors have, from time to time, expressed concern that what they are sharing may be premature because it is merely "drafts" of our final reporting system. However, as lifelong learners, we have had to admit that all of our current teaching strategies are merely "drafts" of what will come later as we learn more. We hope that you will find our thoughts on reporting systems valuable stimuli to your own inquiry into ways to make reporting systems more meaningful to students, parents, and teachers.

Acknowledgments

The belief system that serves as the foundation for all of the endeavors in which we engage is influenced by so many people that it is virtually impossible to be consciously aware of all of those who have contributed. Kathy Short and Carolyn Burke (1991), in their book *Creating Curriculum: Teachers and Students as a Community of Learners* (Portsmouth, NH: Heinemann), call such influences "natural thought collectives" (pg. vii). We find this term to be especially descriptive of those who have influenced and illuminated our thinking. Essential growth experiences for us have been our memberships in IRA, NCTE, Whole Language Umbrella, and Kansas-TAWL. Less formal, but no less important have been professional development groups within our university and school district and extensive conversations with caring, knowledgeable colleagues. Additionally, the writings of many people have influenced our thinking. Books by Heinemann authors in the area of language and curriculum have greatly influenced us as can be seen by the numerous citations at the ends of chapters.

However, there are some people who have made specific contributions to this work. Sandy Rickets and Gordon Gulseth have shared their experiences and thinking as classroom teacher and building administrator. Juan Sexton, Brad and Marlene Dietz, Gloria Doyle, and Cliff and Billie Hall shared their perspectives as parents of elementary students. Bonnie Campbell-Hill, author, and Sue Canavan of Christopher-Gordon Publishers, Inc. have shared their thinking and materials with us. The authors of the various chapters have written, listened to our concerns, and rewritten the material several times.

As we worked to complete this book, we discovered that writing the words was only the first and in some cases the easiest step. The actual assembling of all of the bits and pieces into one unified whole was a tremendous task. It could not have been accomplished without the careful attention to detail and patience of Geri Krier and her staff, particularly Debbie Mulsow of Word Processing at Emporia State University.

We would be remiss if we did not talk about the contributions made by our families. Not only did our husbands and children assume additional duties to free our time and our minds to concentrate on this project, they also took us away from the project at critical moments so that we might retain a balance in our lives.

We anxiously await the comments of our colleagues as they receive our work. Their comments and ideas will help us continue our journey of discovery.

Section One

IMPLICATIONS OF REPORTING SYSTEMS

Chapter 1
Messages About Learning

TARA AZWELL

The purpose of education is to transmit the culture of the community to future generations. That culture consists of beliefs about such things as what is true and what is valuable. Educational systems attempt to transmit community customs and mores to future generations. The fact that educational systems have varied widely around the world is testament to the fact that expectations about the purposes and practices of schools are closely related to the cultural expectations and values of the various communities.

The purpose of assessment, evaluation, and reporting systems is to provide accurate feedback to learners about the state of their learning. The opinions of both learners and others are important in this process. Such information is vital so that learners can make rational judgments about the accuracy of their knowledge and the level of their performance. The information, even when outside observers disagree about its accuracy, is the raw material learners use to self-assess and evaluate their own performance. Self-assessment and evaluation are the essential processes in creating lifelong learners. Reporting systems must effectively transmit the information to interested parties.

Information about the accuracy of knowledge and the level of performance is also of interest to those responsible for helping learners develop the knowledge and skills required to be successful members of the community. Therefore, parents, teachers, and others are aided in their decision-making activities when they possess information about what learners know and can do.

A LOOK AT EVALUATION AND REPORTING

Report cards and letter and number grading systems have grown out of a paradigm of education stemming from the time of the industrial revolution in the 1700s. Some of the beliefs underlying the paradigm include the following:

- The purpose of schools is to create a literate work force.
- A certain set of facts exists that all students must master to be "educated."
- Only certain students have the potential to benefit from schooling; others must be identified and channeled into other training.
- All students begin at the same point in their learning and are capable of learning at the same rate if they work hard enough.
- The teacher is responsible for supplying the information, holding students accountable for learning, and measuring their success.
- The student is responsible for working hard and learning the identified material.
- Students who do not learn the material in the given amount of time are either not working hard enough or are incapable of learning. They should either repeat the process or be removed from the program.

During the Industrial Revolution, the rudiments of education were deemed desirable for the masses, even though true universal education did not exist. The poor, the handicapped, and women were normally excluded. Basic education was needed for religious reasons and to provide citizens who could earn a living and contribute to "democratic" society.

Higher levels of education were only for those who demonstrated academic talent. Academic talent was often defined as the ability to memorize facts; to engage in convergent thinking and problem solving; to work hard; to be docile, cooperative, and respectful; and perhaps to pay. The privilege of receiving higher levels of education led to management jobs in business, or professional careers. Generally the more schooling one had, the more money one was likely to make. Social status in the community was often related to the amount of formal schooling one had. Thus, continuing in school for longer periods of time carried significant rewards.

Formalized evaluation and reporting systems were developed to sort and categorize students. Students who did not meet preset standards of performance were excluded from advanced schooling by being forced to repeat a lower level or having to leave school. Students were motivated to continue school because of monetary and positional rewards associated with attaining higher levels of schooling. Losing the privilege of attending school meant entering the work force in often low status and low-paying positions.

In the United States, periodic exams were given. Students wrote essays, worked problems, and supplied factual answers to questions to demonstrate their mastery of required material. Those who did well were allowed to continue their education, while those who did not meet the standard were denied access to further education. Numerous numerical and letter grading systems were developed to define the level of performance. Behavioral scientists and statisticians conducted research to determine the averages and ranges of many aspects of human behavior. Norms, measures of central tendency, measures of deviation from the mean, percentiles, and other statistics were developed to track group and individual performance. Objectivity, reliability, and validity became issues of concern requiring complex mathematical calculations to remove personal opinion and bias from evaluation. Data that could be translated into numbers was often the primary data on which evaluation was based.

A NEW PARADIGM OF EDUCATION

During the 1900s, researchers began to ask questions that reflected some new insights into learning. Most teachers still believe that schools should create a literate, productive work force. Teachers are responsible for presenting important information. Students must work hard to learn. However, other beliefs of the older paradigm are being questioned. With information increasing dramatically, it is becoming increasingly difficult to identify a particular body of knowledge that must be mastered by all. Today, helping students to become lifelong learners who are capable of accessing the information they need appears to be more promising than requiring them to memorize by rote a certain body of facts. Researchers have also begun to define learning as a continuum occurring from birth to death, with learning never totally lacking or totally accomplished (Azwell 1994). Terms such as *emergent learning, developing learning,* and *proficient application* are often used.

Researchers and theorists have identified other factors about learning that have greatly influenced our paradigm of schools (Cambourne 1988; Goodman 1986; Halliday 1973).

- Learners learn how to do something when they need to do that thing for a real purpose.
- Because function precedes form, no preexisting sequence of learning exists, although some general patterns of learning can be identified.

- Learners are responsible for their own learning because they decide what they will learn and when.
- Teachers increase the probability that learning will take place by having high expectations, demonstrating why the information is valuable, modeling strategies for learning, and providing feedback while accepting beginning attempts to learn.
- Learners learn at different rates.
- There is little correlation between learning quickly and performing well.
- Time is a critical factor in learning, and most learners can achieve the desired level of performance if given adequate time.

The views just described have influenced our understanding of how learning occurs and what the function of the school should be. Beliefs about the purpose of school have broadened such that schools exist not only to prepare students for the adult world of work but also to help them become thinking members of a global society, to develop their individual abilities to a high level, and to enable them to become caring, contributing members of the community.

We know that students of the same age are at varying points along the learning continuum. Mission statements declare that all children can learn. Teachers realize that grade-level scores and grade-level curricula organize material viewed as important. In real classrooms, children of similar ages perform in widely differing ways on different tasks. Some schools have even begun to question the advisability of organizing children into classes on the basis of age. Multi-age classrooms are being developed in many communities.

Because of changes in belief systems, instructional strategies have changed significantly. Teachers no longer rely on textbooks to determine the appropriate curriculum for students. State mandates have encouraged school districts to determine developmentally appropriate learning outcomes for students in their schools (Kansas State Board of Education 1991). Teachers have been actively involved in the process. Benchmark statements describe expectations for students at each level of school. From benchmark statements, teachers have identified learning goals for their classrooms and have written indicators, descriptors, and/or standards of performance. Various levels of performance from pre-emergent through proficient and accelerated levels have been described.

The strategies teachers use to help students achieve these goals have also changed. No longer do students simply listen to lectures, read the textbook and answer questions, work pages of problems, and take paper-and-pencil tests. Teachers employ many hands-on, process-oriented methods of teaching. Students participate in literature response groups, writing workshops, and investigations in math, science, and social studies. They work individually, in pairs, in cooperative groups, and as whole classes. Teachers no longer view themselves as "givers of wisdom" but as learners with more experience who have insights to share with fellow learners. Teachers serve as models, demonstrators, facilitators, questioners, reflectors, encouragers, as well as instructors.

NEED FOR A NEW PARADIGM OF REPORTING SYSTEMS

Only recently have our assessment and evaluation systems begun to change to reflect our new understanding of the learning continuum and the implementation of a broader range of instructional strategies (Dismuke 1993). We now seek information about a student's learning in an ongoing, multifaceted approach that includes observations of the processes and product, self-evaluations, as well as more traditional tests.

An elementary classroom teacher describes her frustration with traditional reporting systems this way:

> Are you reinventing the grade card every nine weeks? That is how I have often felt when preparing grade cards. Admittedly it is my own fault. After all, my district has a card that requires only a grade and a few boxes filled in per subject. My district, and most parents, would feel that I had fulfilled my obligations by filling out that card. I do not. To me, there is an implied responsibility to inform the parents of their child's abilities and achievements. That grade and a few boxes don't do the job adequately.
>
> The reporting process seems to be missing the point entirely. Reporting should be more than just a quick "dip sticking." We would resent a doctor who presumed to give us our entire health report after a single pulse and temperature check. Wouldn't we demand more than a mere "OK" or "Not OK"? Wouldn't we demand the right to at least know what an OK meant?
>
> I see the role of a "good teacher" as very much like that of a "good doctor." Teachers need to be able to show what the student's skills and needs are. We also need to prescribe for their future educational "good health." To do this we must have a way to picture a student's current status and where they are going. A good grading/reporting system could do this.
>
> Over the years I have found ways to improve my teaching methods and ways of gathering information. I collect specific, detailed data for each child that enables me to picture that child for the parents in a much more satisfactory way.
>
> It boils down to Double Duty. I am busily squirreling away lots of wonderful information about my students. It is specific and quite detailed. But when I am ready to send all this good stuff home, there is no place on the grade card to put many of the important areas.
>
> I don't know how other teachers feel, but anytime I send out an official report with my name attached, it is the equivalent of a legal document. The

information on that report declares itself to be the best and latest educational information on a child. This may sound overly dramatic, but parents are expecting that report to tell them about an important chunk of their child's life. It is supposed to be true, and it is official.

Sandra Ricketts
Fourth-grade teacher

In the past, educators placed so much reliance on number- and letter-grade performance evaluations that the general public believed that it knew what grades, percentages, grade-level equivalences, and percentiles meant. While such concepts appear to be simple—an A is 94–100 percent—they are often much more complicated. Two complicating conditions exist. Not all As represent 94–100 percent. Some As are 90–100 percent or some other percentage. Even if the exact percentages are known, this does not tell what material was covered or by what means of measurement the percentages were determined.

Grades also appear on first view to be "objective" and fair. Each learner is given the same opportunity to master the same materials. In practice, this is not the case. Students bring to the learning situation differing amounts of prior knowledge about the material. Students learn at widely varying rates and through different learning styles. Teaching styles vary greatly and do not accommodate the learning styles uniformly. The designer of the "objective" measure acts in a subjective manner in selecting which part of the material to test, what types of responses to require, how much time to allow, and many other factors. All teachers and test makers do not decide in the same way. Teachers often vary their own procedures from class to class, student to student, or year to year based on their expectations. Therefore, a "94–100 percent A" in one class might represent a very different level of performance from a "94–100 percent A" in another class.

The evaluation system we use also ignores another fact of learning that educators have come to recognize. Although students learn or perform at different rates, the rate of learning does not determine the ultimate level of competence. The goal of education is to reach an acceptable level of competence. A very good example of this principle is a child learning to speak. Some children begin speaking around twelve months of age, whereas others are three years old before they talk well enough to be understood by others. However, most children possess at least minimally acceptable levels of oral competence when they reach school age. In fact, some of the children who did not talk much before age three develop high levels of oral communication skills.

Evaluation and reporting systems used most frequently in our schools today measure all students after the same period of learning time. Often on the basis of one-time measures, this system identifies those who have mastered the measured tasks as competent, and those who are still working to master the tasks as incompetent even though the latter may eventually become as competent or even more competent than their faster-learning peers. Because evaluation measures look at just a small sample of the behavior, a true picture of the level of competence often is obscured, and the student, teacher, parent, and others needing accurate feedback about levels of achievement are misled.

THE PURPOSE OF THIS BOOK

At conferences, at in-service training sessions, and in the professional literature, educators are expressing concern that the percentage and letter-grade grading systems used in many districts make it very difficult for teachers to express what they know about the progress and achievement of their students. Because of these concerns, educators are looking for new ways to communicate information about student achievement to all parties responsible for helping students become competent learners. Among those with vested interests in the learning process are students, parents, teachers, administrators, state officials, and future employers.

The purpose of this book is to share some of the ways educators are addressing their concerns. Many of the processes described require major shifts in paradigms. What does it mean to learn, to teach, and to be a competent, lifelong learner who can fulfill the responsibilities of a contributing member of the community?

The following chapters attempt to answer questions such as these:

- What are the effects of current grading and reporting systems on all of the children in our schools today, including special needs students and students from diverse backgrounds?
- How can teachers and schools desiring to change their reporting systems undertake the task?
- What are some possible ways to report student achievement without using traditional grades and report cards?
- What are some facets of changing grading and reporting systems that educators must consider as they attempt to improve their own systems?

The authors of this book do not have definitive answers. We have simply begun to ask what we consider to be significant questions. Each day we revise, expand, and refine our answers. We invite you to join us on the journey.

REFERENCES

Azwell, T. 1994. "A New Look at Report Cards." *The Kansas Journal of Reading,* in press.

Cambourne, B. 1988. *The Whole Story.* Auckland, NZ: Ashton-Scholastic.

Dismuke, D. 1993. "Are Report Cards Obsolete?" *NEA Today* 11 (9):12–13.

Goodman, K. 1986. *What's Whole in Whole Language?* Portsmouth, NH: Heinemann.

Halliday, M. 1973. *Explorations in Functions of Language.* New York: Elsevier.

Kansas State Board of Education 1991. *Kansas Quality Performance Accreditation: A Plan for Living, Learning and Working in a Global Society.* Topeka, KS: KSBE.

Chapter 2
Report Card Options for Students with Disabilities in General Education

TES A. MEHRING

A major area of concern for general education teachers is the reporting of student progress using a monthly, quarterly, or semiannual report card. This process takes on even greater importance when the report card is being developed for one or more mainstreamed students with disabilities. Schulz and Turnbull (1984) stated, "The preparation of report cards is among the most difficult tasks performed by the classroom teacher. The evaluation dilemma is even more complex for students with disabilities who require specially designed instruction in the regular classroom. The challenge for educators is to devise fair reporting systems that accomplish the purpose of evaluation while considering the interests of both handicapped and non-handicapped students" (126).

In addition to being difficult for teachers, the use of traditional report cards to report the academic progress of students with disabilities has received criticism from varied sources. According to Retish, Horvath, Hitchings, and Schmalle (1991), traditional grading and reporting systems do not adequately reflect the intent of Public Law 94-142 (Education of All Handicapped Children Act, 1975) or Public Law 101-476 (Individuals with Disabilities Education Act, 1990) to individualize instructional systems for students with disabilities. According to these and other authors, the traditional system of comparing an individual with a disability with the rest of the class is no longer appropriate. As more and more districts pursue the regular education initiative (the integration of students with mild disabilities into general education) or full inclusion (the placement of *all* students with disabilities into general education), there is little merit in verifying through the use of traditional report cards that students with disabilities may not perform as well as other students.

Parkay (1982) asserted that traditional report cards encourage student passivity and dishonesty, increase teacher-student confrontations, and erode students' sense of self-worth. Traditional report cards have also been criticized for their unreliability and inaccuracy. "In most cases, teachers who distribute report card grades on an absolute basis (grades of A–F or numerical rating systems) lack an adequate frame of reference for making such judgments. In any event, such marks typically reflect adjusted percentage-correct scores on some poorly defined hodgepodge of learning tasks" (Gronlund 1974, 32).

Other, more temperate critics feel that some form of reporting student progress to parents four to six times each year through the use of report cards is an essential feature of the curriculum and that complete abolition of report cards is realistic only up to a point (Gage & Berliner 1991; Good & Brophy 1990). Thus, the number of educators who stress the need to improve, not abolish, present report card practices, especially for students with disabilities in mainstream classes, continues to grow.

There is no "best" system to handle the complexities of reporting academic progress for students with disabilities, especially those who are achieving significantly below grade level. Any serious discussion about the use of report cards with students with disabilities must address three key questions:

1. Have the letter or numerical marks listed on traditional report cards been determined through daily or weekly activities that allow students with disabilities to accurately display knowledge about the course content?
2. Can traditional report cards be adapted to communicate the progress of students with disabilities more accurately and fairly?
3. Do alternatives to traditional report cards exist?

The remainder of this chapter examines the answers to these questions.

TRADITIONAL REPORT CARD USE

In most schools, report card grades are established by comparing the student's achievement to that of a peer group. The report card format is generally established by the school system with little regard for the underlying need for meaningful communication between student and teacher or teacher and parent. Teachers who must conform to prescribed report card policies and procedures are often in a dilemma concerning fair treatment of mainstreamed students.

Designing a fair reporting system for students with disabilities must begin with an analysis of how traditional report card marks are determined. Letter- or number-grade report cards are the most widely used reporting systems in K–12 classrooms (Good & Brophy 1990). The specific mark assigned to a student for an academic subject is usually based on a percentage or frequency count calculated for written daily assignments and tests. Such noncorrective feedback focuses on a student's response accuracy and leads to efficiency in computing marks for traditional report cards. A major concern with this practice is that many students, especially those with disabilities, have significant difficulty demonstrating the true depth of knowledge they possess on written tasks. If traditional report cards must be used, teachers should consider accommodations in instruction and student assessment that will promote a more accurate reflection of student knowledge in the marks assigned.

Instructional Accommodations

Various accommodations for individual differences can be made in the instructional process. Gloeckler and Simpson (1988) described four specific strategies to improve the performance of students with disabilities:

1. Students who are slow workers but not slow learners can be given additional time to complete worksheets and other assignments. Also, the number of math problems or written sentences in language arts can be reduced. These measures will help ensure that the grade is based on knowledge of the material rather than on the time it takes to complete the task.

2. Students with written language difficulties can be graded on oral responses.

3. Students who have conceptual difficulties can be given a choice of topics for oral or written reports.

4. A teacher can use more than one text in a class. The use of supplementary books will allow students to use texts appropriate to their reading level. When a topic is assigned, students read the text and prepare for class discussion.

Teachers can also use cooperative learning and multitechnology presentations to help students with disabilities integrate important concepts and content, and acquire skills.

Accommodations in Assessing Student Knowledge

In grading tests, teachers must be able to distinguish between students' knowledge of subject content and their ability to produce answers in the test's format. Students may have difficulty understanding the questions, following directions on items such as matching or filling in the blanks, reading test questions, or writing the answers. Students with disabilities may also do poorly owing to test anxiety. If the grade is to accurately represent what they have learned, students should not be penalized for difficulties in these areas.

The following actions are recommended to assist students in taking tests:

- Directions, although written, should be read aloud, and students should be given the opportunity to ask questions.
- Students who work slowly should be given extra time.
- When appropriate, tests should be given in the resource room, where students with visual-perception difficulties can receive individual assistance with matching or filling in all the blanks.
- Resource room teachers or tutors should read the test questions and write the responses if the students cannot.
- When appropriate, teachers should prerecord the questions on a cassette. Students would work at a listening center with earphones, stopping the tape after each question as they write their answers.

In addition, teachers may want to consider measuring the progress of all students through the use of authentic or performance-based measurements rather than paper-and-pencil tasks. Authentic assessments may include one or more of the following:

- direct observation of student behavior
- checklists and anecdotal records
- student interviews and surveys
- individual projects
- videotapes and audiotapes
- cooperative group and class projects
- class interaction and discussion
- verbal reports
- logs and journals
- simulations and dramatizations
- portfolios

- modified tests that emphasize verbal and/or written performance
- debates

Authentic assessments allow teachers to observe what students know and what they can do with the information acquired. Authentic assessments provide students with disabilities the opportunity to demonstrate what they have learned using formats that promote rather than penalize their knowledge base.

Traditional report cards *can* be used to report the progress of students with disabilities in general education classrooms. Teachers must ensure, however, that the marks assigned reflect accurate observations of student knowledge. Accommodations in instruction and daily or weekly assessment of student knowledge are essential.

TRADITIONAL REPORT CARD ADAPTATIONS

If district policy allows, teachers may want to consider using one or more "adaptations" of traditional report cards. Adaptations include pass-fail grades; effort grades; student progress grades; dual marking systems (achievement and ability grades); and supplementary progress reports. Following is a brief explanation of each of these adaptations.

Pass-Fail

A fairly simple report card adaptation, the pass-fail system requires a teacher to specify minimum competencies for a course or field of study. Students who meet or exceed the benchmark competencies receive a "pass." Likewise, students who do not demonstrate minimal competence receive a "failing" grade on the report card. The pass-fail report card option reduces anxiety for students, relieves teachers of comparative evaluations of student work, reduces competition among students, and identifies critical outcomes that students must achieve to pass a course. The drawback to the pass-fail report card procedure is that some students may not put forth the same degree of effort that they would if "traditional" report card grades were being used.

Effort Grades

In addition to traditional marks for quality of performance in academic subjects, a supplemental mark can be used to indicate how much effort the student has exhibited. Marks of E (excellent), S (satisfactory), or U (unsatisfactory) or 1 (best effort), 2 (good effort but could work harder), or 3 (poor effort-needs improvement) can be assigned. The use of effort grades can provide additional information about the progress and work habits of students with disabilities. For example, a fourth-grade student who receives a D in reading but an E effort grade is reading below average but putting forth maximum effort in comparison to peers. The teacher and parents may want to explore tutoring, the use of different methods of instruction, and/or the use of materials more appropriate to the student's ability level.

Student Progress Grades

Another adaptation that can supplement the traditional report card is the inclusion of student progress grades for students with disabilities. Progress grades are similar to effort grades but focus on student progress in each area:

S - progress is satisfactory
I - progress is improving
N - progress needs improvement
U - progress is unsatisfactory

Although probably not as informative as effort grades, progress grades can communicate useful information to parents and students.

Dual Marking Systems

Some schools have elected to post two marks for each subject area for students with disabilities. Traditional marks are used to represent student performance in comparison to peers (achievement) and according to ability. The report card might look something like the following:

	Achievement	Ability
Language Arts	C	A
Mathematics	D	A
Science	D	B
Social Studies	C	B

Mastery of stated criteria becomes the basis for assigning ability grades. For instance, in language arts, students might be expected to proofread their written work for capitalization, punctuation, and spelling errors. A student with disabilities in this class might have a stated criterion of proofreading for capitalization errors only. Ability grades are assigned using the following scale:

A - performance exceeds the stated criterion
B - performance is slightly above the stated criterion
C - performance meets the stated criterion
D - performance is slightly below the stated criterion
F - performance is significantly below the stated criterion

Supplementary Progress Reports

A final adaptation that can accompany traditional report cards is the supplementary progress report. The progress report is a written narrative that more fully explains a student's academic and/or behavioral performance during a given reporting period. A progress report for an eighth-grade student with a learning disability in an eighth-grade editing class might look something like this:

> Alphonso has improved his ability to recognize and correct spelling errors. He has mastered the recognition and capitalization of proper nouns, names, titles, and buildings. He is not yet consistent in his capitalization of cities. Punctuation, especially the use of commas, is also an area in which Alphonso needs improvement. He has been using the computer to prepare drafts of his written products. This has made it easier for him to edit since his handwriting is laborious and illegible at times. The overall quality and length of his creative writings has improved significantly since the last reporting period. We will continue to focus on capitalization and punctuation throughout the next grading period. In addition, we will begin working on recognizing and correcting sentence problems (fragments, run-ons, unclear pronoun reference, and awkward sentences).

TRADITIONAL REPORT CARD ALTERNATIVES

Some school districts are designing report cards that recognize individual differences in intellectual ability and learning strength. Such report cards provide descriptive information about a student's accomplishment of specific learning outcomes or performance objectives for a grade level or course. In addition, these report cards illustrate individual student gains and identify areas needing improvement. Contracts, progress checklists, and portfolios are alternatives to traditional report cards currently being used by some school districts to report student progress. Each can be used for quarterly or semester reporting periods.

Contracts

Contracts are one of the most widely used alternatives to determine and report the progress of students with disabilities in the regular classroom. A contract is a written agreement between the classroom teacher and student that specifies a level of performance the student must maintain to obtain a specific grade. Retish, Horvath, Hitchings, and Schmalle (1991, 152) specified several components that should be included in a contract:

- type(s) of work to be completed by the student
- quality of work to be completed by the student
- statement of how the quality of work will be determined
- signature of the involved parties (for example, general education teacher, student, special education teacher, or parent)
- timelines (if appropriate) for completion of the work

Contracts should be clearly written in language that is easily understood by the student and should be developed *prior* to the beginning of instruction. Figure 2–1 provides an illustration of a sample contract.

Progress Checklists

Progress or competency checklists are widely used in skill-oriented courses and in developmentally sequenced courses (for example, mathematics and vocational auto mechanics). Competencies for a checklist are derived from course goals, outcomes, and/or objectives. Goals and objectives on the student's Individual Educational Program (IEP) could also provide the competencies for the checklist. Checklists list skills and concepts taught in each subject area for the period of time covered by the reporting schedule. Columns can be provided for the teacher to indicate whether each skill or concept has been "mastered" or "still needs improvement." Hill and Ruptic (1994) have expanded the evaluation continuum to include the following options for commenting on student progress: beginning, expanding, fluent, proficient, and independent. Figure 2–2 is an example of a progress checklist that could be used for an elementary education student.

Schulz and Turnbull (1984) listed several advantages of progress checklists: "The reporting system is clearly based on the substance of the student's curriculum; parents and students are provided with specific information on skill development indicating the progress the student is making and the areas needing more concentrated effort; information derived from the checklist can assist parents in selecting skills and concepts to practice/reinforce at home" (37). A key disadvantage of checklists is that stu-

---

Sample Contract

This is a contract between _____ and _____

for Algebra 1. Those who have signed this agreement below agree that listed assignments will be completed by the agreed upon date and will meet all specific requirements listed below. If the terms of the contract are met by the student, the student will receive the points listed toward the final grade in this class.

Assignment	Completion Date	Specific Requirements	Evaluation Comments
1.			
2.			
3.			
4.			

Student Signature	**Date**
Teacher Signature	**Date**

Figure 2–1 *Sample Contract*

dents with disabilities may be embarrassed if a checklist approach is not being used for nondisabled students. Also, checklists do not easily translate into the calculation of grade point averages.

Portfolios

A classroom portfolio is "an organized collection of student work and self-reflections that helps paint a portrait of the whole child" (Hill & Ruptic 1994). Portfolios can range from simple to very comprehensive collections of student work. They can include videotapes, audiotapes, writing samples, workbook pages, surveys, checklists, anecdotal records, tests, and student self-reflections. Student products included in the portfolio can be best work, works in progress, pieces the student is most proud of or worked the

Progress Checklist

	Objectives	Mastered	Needs Improvement	Comments
1.	Identify and use capital letters in outlines.	_____	_____	_____
2.	Demonstrate ability to produce punctuation symbols for period, question mark, exclamation mark, comma, apostrophe, quotation marks, underlining, hyphen, and colon.	_____	_____	_____
3.	Identify and place a period after all abbreviations used with addresses (*Rd., Ave., Blvd., Dr., Rte., Apt., P.O. Box*).	_____	_____	_____
4.	Identify and place an apostrophe in all contractions (*you've, couldn't*).	_____	_____	_____
5.	Identify and place a hyphen in a fraction (*one-fifth*).	_____	_____	_____
6.	Identify and use singular and plural pronouns (*Mary went to the library. She checked out two books. Bill and Jim are excited. They are going to the circus*).	_____	_____	_____
7.	Identify and use adverbs.	_____	_____	_____
8.	Identify and write an exclamatory sentence (*Be careful!*).	_____	_____	_____
9.	Write a compound (combining) sentence using a comma and the words *and, but,* or *or* (*We could go to the movie, or we could play tennis*).	_____	_____	_____
10.	Order sentences in a paragraph using the words *first, next, then, finally.*	_____	_____	_____

Figure 2–2 *Progress Checklist*

hardest on, or those completed at the beginning and end of the reporting period. Portfolios can include student- and/or teacher-selected samples of student performance. Students should be active participants in the construction of the portfolio. They should be informed at the beginning of the year about what should be included in the portfolio and how it will be evaluated. Portfolios allow teachers, students, and parents to observe ongoing progress. The key disadvantage is that portfolios do not easily translate into the calculation of grade point averages.

SUMMARY

The design and use of judicious and meaningful report cards for students with disabilities, especially those included within general education, can be a difficult task. The traditional system of comparing a student with a disability with the rest of the class is inconsistent with the goals of the Education of All Handicapped Children Act and the Individuals with Disabilities Education Act. Accommodations in instruction and assessment of student progress can promote a more accurate representation of student knowledge when traditional report cards are used. Adaptations of and alternatives to traditional report cards also provide effective ways to report the academic progress of students with disabilities. The system selected should recognize individual differences in intellectual ability and learning strength for *all* students. Report cards should provide descriptive information illustrating student accomplishments and identify areas needing improvement. Accommodations in instruction, testing, and/or the grading process itself can reduce teachers' stress in assigning grades and increase the relevance of report cards for parents and their students with disabilities.

REFERENCES

Gage, N. L., and D. C. Berliner. 1991. *Educational Psychology.* 5th ed. Boston, MA: Houghton Mifflin Company.

Gloeckler, T., and C. Simpson. 1988. *Exceptional Students in Regular Classrooms: Challenges, Services, and Methods.* Mountain View, CA: Mayfield Publishing Company.

Good, T., and J. Brophy. 1990. *Educational Psychology.* 4th ed. New York, NY: Longman.

Gronlund, N. E. 1974. *Improving Marking and Reporting in Classroom Instruction.* New York, NY: Macmillan.

Hill, B. C., and C. Ruptic. 1994. *Practical Aspects of Authentic Assessment: Putting the Pieces Together.* Norwood, MA: Christopher Gordon Publishers, Inc.

Parkay, F. 1982. "The Success-Oriented Curriculum." *The Clearing House* 61 (2): 66–68.

Retish, P., M. Horvath, W. Hitchings, and B. Schmalle. 1991. *Students with Mild Disabilities in the Secondary School.* New York, NY: Longman.

Schulz, J., and A. Turnbull. 1984. *Mainstreaming Handicapped Students.* Boston, MA: Allyn and Bacon, Inc.

Chapter 3
Communicating in a Culturally Diverse Community

EILEEN HOGAN

Students who start school with a language other than English will make up nearly 18 percent of all students by the turn of the century (Conklin & Lauri 1983). Teachers facing the blank stares of students who may represent three to ten languages other than English or come from different ethnic groups are justifiably frustrated. Knowing how to teach, assess, and report such students' learning is a daunting task. Children from diverse backgrounds and those whose learning style differs from that expected by the teacher may suffer by being left on the periphery of the learning community. Great emphasis has been placed on the differing needs of such children and various strategies to help them achieve. Actually, a sensitive, flexible approach to teaching and assessment will benefit *all* children. An outwardly homogenous group may have as much diversity in ability, personality, and learning style as a group with obvious ethnic differences. So, although this chapter is geared toward the multicultural implications of assessment, many or most of the strategies described can benefit all children.

Instructional strategies have been steeped in traditional pencil-and-paper seat work. Research conducted during the past ten years clearly shows that children learn best through a variety of activities and methods. Likewise, assessment of children's abilities is still rooted in report cards that are given to parents three or four times a year. Educators are questioning traditional reporting systems. They find that the single letter grade or numerical score does not reflect what they know about a child. However, it is still most common that one letter represents all of a student's work in one area. Some forms provide room for a short note about study habits and some only have room for a signature.

In the traditional report card format, letters and other marks typically overemphasize work habits and discrete academic skills: works independently, works neatly, follows directions, or has worked twenty-five math problems correctly. Yet important areas of creativity, flexibility, and problem solving aren't even addressed on the forms (Shedlin 1988). The traditional reports are based on nonproductive peer comparisons rather than meaningful descriptions of a particular child's progress over time (Freeman & Hatch 1989).

The standard report card format also does not facilitate home-school communication. Parents are asked only to provide a signature that verifies the card has been received. This is not an effective use of a tool that could greatly enhance communication (Ediger 1982). Many parents are comfortable with the traditional report card and do not expect to see "grades" in creativity, flexibility, and problem solving. Teachers who have changed their reporting system have had to teach parents about the advantages of the new system and have found reactions that varied from enthusiasm to indifference to hostility. Yet all teachers know that parent cooperation and involvement is key to enhancing a child's education.

Although numerous strategies exist to encourage parental involvement, this is particularly difficult to achieve with diverse populations. However, it is not advisable to provide a list or "recipe" of activities to use when interacting with specific groups. To do so merely perpetuates stereotypes. Racial and ethnic affiliation do not always determine beliefs, values, and perceptions.

Any strategy that respectfully seeks each family's input or help will be more successful than one that assumes that a single approach will work with all members of a particular group. For example, the assumption that in Hispanic families, the mother or wife stays in the background and all communication must be directed to the father or husband is stereotypic and may not be true. It is best to treat each family individually, regardless of its ethnic group or social status.

The types of questions used to elicit responses from parents determine the type of information obtained. Open-ended questions, of course, elicit more detailed information than yes-or-no questions. For example, asking (through a translator if necessary), "What language do you speak at home with your children?" is better than asking, "Do you speak English at home?"

It is also important (and just plain courteous) to make every attempt to pronounce names correctly. Americans are woefully tongue-tied when it comes to non-European names. Be up front and ask the family member to repeat names slowly and several times if necessary. Try saying, "My ears are not used to hearing different names; please help me say yours correctly." This works well for both children and parents.

Children who immigrate after beginning school in their home country often experience a downward spiral in U.S. schools. Teaching strategies and report cards immersed in the values of schools different from those of the families pose barriers to these children in addition to the language barrier (Mounts 1986).

So what are the alternatives? The traditional report card system has been around so long and is so well entrenched that it is difficult to change (Hall 1989). Portfolios are the most common alternative to traditional report cards and can provide a successful system for reporting children's progress in school. The contents of portfolios vary based on their purpose and audience. There are numerous resources describing ways to develop effective portfolios. Following are other reporting systems that effectively communicate to families what children from diverse backgrounds can do.

PERFORMANCE ASSESSMENT

Performance assessment is not new. Rather, it is common in the fields of law, medicine, and industry. A system of assessment and reporting, performance assessment must satisfy three criteria. First, students must apply knowledge they have acquired. Secondly, students must complete a task with a real or simulated setting. And finally, students must demonstrate proficiency in performing the task or creating a product, a process that must be observed and rated by trained observers. (Pierson & Beck 1987).

Teachers can make use of either structured or spontaneous performance assessments. Using both is the best approach (Stiggins & Bridgeford 1986). The value of teachers' day-to-day abilities to observe students is universally acknowledged. In addition, teachers should structure performance assessment to meet standards of reliability and validity, and plan for a specific purpose.

Examples:

Unstructured: The teacher observes that a child measures the length of several objects in the room using a variety of measuring units (string, tape measure, pencil length, or her whole body).
Structured: The teacher provides a child with several objects such as those listed above and asks the child to measure the table with two of

them. It is a valid and reliable way to assess the child's ability to use measurement.

Both of these types of assessment are at home in a portfolio of work. They can both be written succinctly and explained along with other evidence of math ability (Pierson and Beck 1987).

CHECKLISTS

Many sources on portfolios suggest that a comprehensive checklist is an integral part of the entire assessment package for students (Grace & Shores 1991). The advantage of checklists is that parents can readily understand them and they avoid some of the drawbacks of individual grades, such as competition, comparison, and being singular in focus (Hall 1989). For more information about these kinds of report forms, see Chapter 11.

Checklists can also be effective communication tools (Gullo 1994). Figure 3–1 shows a checklist that focuses on broad developmental and achievement-oriented behaviors within six main areas of learner achievement. It does not focus on specific skills like letter recognition, vocabulary words, or counting. It does require the teacher to rate each area over time.

Checklists can also be developed that communicate information about a child's level of performance in both the primary and secondary language (see Figure 3–2).

NARRATIVE REPORTS

The narrative report not only offers the teacher a way to show a particular child's progress, it also provides an opportunity to explain the curriculum and performance expectations to the family (Horm-Wingerd 1992, 12). To be effective, the narrative report must be clear and succinct and easily understood by the parents. Teachers find it easiest to follow an outline of topics in the curriculum or broad developmental domains (Bredekamp 1987). The Albermarle County (Virginia) Schools (1990a, 1990b) suggest that narrative reports include the following components:

- Specific examples of what a child can do. These avoid vague comments or detailed descriptions. Teachers should emphasize strengths, capabilities, and what individual children can do.
- Descriptions of meaningful, relevant behavior. These are based on teacher observations of children interacting with objects and peers in

	Emergent Developing Competent		
COMMUNICATIONS	Beginning of Term	Mid-Term	End of Term
Speaking: Children will demonstrate the ability to:			
• Ask questions and answer questions of others.			
• Convey information to others.			
• Use language to solve problems.			
• Participate in a variety of oral language activities.			
• Share thoughts and understanding with an attentive audience.			
• State and support opinions.			
Listening: Children will demonstrate the ability to:			
• Understand a spoken message.			
• Respond appropriately to what they heard.			
• Focus on the speaker.			
• Recognize purposes for listening.			
Writing: Children will demonstrate the ability to:			
• Use developmentally appropriate forms of writing.			
• Use a variety of writing tools and equipment.			
• Express written thoughts on self-selected topics.			
• Write across the curriculum.			
• Observe and demonstrate the connecting of spoken and written language.			
• Acquire and extend writing skills.			
• Publish selected compositions.			
Reading: Children will demonstrate the ability to:			
• Read varied genre of children's literature.			
• Read own compositions.			
• Read across the curriculum.			
• Acquire reading skills at appropriate levels.			

Figure 3–1 *Communications Checklist*

Writing Checklist

Student _____   Year _____
Teacher _____   Date of Entry into Classroom _____
Primary Language _____   Secondary Language _____

	DATE	PRIMARY LANGUAGE	SECONDARY LANGUAGE	COMMENTS
Conveys an understandable message				
Self-selects topic				
Uses expansive vocabulary				
Experiments with style				
Uses revision strategies				
WRITING MECHANICS:				
Handwriting				
Uses periods				
Uses question marks				
Uses quotation marks				
Uses exclamation points				
Uses capitalization				
Uses comma/apostrophe/accents				
Grammar usage				
% Invented spelling				
% Conventional spelling				

Figure 3–2 *Writing Checklist*

the typical classroom. Furthermore, there should be a clear link with the program's philosophy and goals.

· Concerns, if any, phrased in a positive way that does not blame the child or the parents. Careful wording is essential. For example, "Following specific directions during work time continues to be a goal for Sarah" is better than "Sarah never does what I ask her to do."

- Goals and plans for the future. These let parents know, for each aspect of the report, exactly what will happen next, and enable them to plan their help. They also educate parents about how young children develop. Some parents may demand a more structured curriculum as well as a traditional reporting system, and the narrative report will answer many of their concerns (Hatch & Freeman 1989; Horm-Wingerd 1992).
- Sensitivity to the emotional impact on parents and children and awareness of the implications for parent-child and home-school relationships. The report should be written so that parents will be able to clearly recognize their child *and* appreciate the amount of teacher input. Shedlin (1988) suggests that such a high-quality report will improve and support communication and trust between parents and teachers. The report will foster further discussions as parents feel more comfortable (Horm-Wingerd 1992).
- Professional preparation and appearance. The report must be technically accurate and polished in appearance. Teachers can ask a colleague to review and critique their reports, paying attention to grammar and appearance. For families whose home language is not English, teachers should request translation services. In fact, for those families used to more informal reports, the translator could give the report orally in the home language while the teacher stands by to answer questions. Figure 3–3 shows a sample narrative report.

It takes conviction and some risk taking to get started. However, once a teacher is convinced of the limitations of the traditional report card, beginning will be easier. Horm-Wingerd (1992) offers a four-step procedure for narrative reports:

1. Open with an overall statement describing a child's progress in broad developmental areas since the last report or conference.
2. Give a specific example of behavior to serve as evidence for your global description of change and to help parents understand exactly what you are describing.
3. State your plans.
4. If appropriate, note what the parents can do at home to facilitate the child's development (14).

Experienced teachers can adjust the procedure as they become accustomed to the process and get to know the parents in their community. A narrative form within outline format (see Figure 3–4) can be developed to provide more structure if desired (McAfee & Leong 1994).

It is important to note that a narrative report is only one type of communication to the parents. Class reports or newsletters, calls, and conferences are all important, and each method has its place in maintaining total con-

Sample Narrative Report

Windemere Elementary School   Date_5/10____

Progress Report

Child__ Jamelah T.___   Class__ 1st grade___
Teacher_ Rowberry___

Jamelah has made great progress in all areas of development this year. Most notable were gains in the area of written language, reading, problem solving and mathematics. At the beginning of the year, Jamelah was printing random letters which she gave meaning to and now she has progressed to writing which conveys her ideas clearly. She writes with a purpose and includes simple details. She uses spaces between words and some capitals and periods. I would expect her to continue to add more details to her writing along with a clearer sense of beginning, middle and ending.

In reading she has progressed from merely retelling a story to reading known and pattern books. She will "read" independently and for at least 15 minutes. If she has the opportunity to both read and be read to this summer she will maintain these skills and improve.

Jamelah now regularly thinks through problems, weighs several alternatives and usually chooses the solution which fits the situation she is in. I would expect her to be able to verbalize why she makes such choices and then try to influence others with her decision.

In math she is correctly counting to 20 by 2's and enjoys adding single digits. She can also use and understand simple graphs. She would benefit from the opportunity to explore sets of many objects so that she can practice counting and combining different amounts. Examples of sets are: spoons, toys, legos, popcorn, buttons, etc.

Jamelah's ability at taking responsibility for her decisions and actions is still developing. Reminders before she begins a new activity have helped her remember to think about the consequences of her actions. Jamelah's science skills are still emerging too. She enjoys observing nature and changes in physical properties yet she needs some careful questioning to help her think things through. Fun outdoor activities with exploration with water, sand and even mud will enhance this skill.

Figure 3–3 *Sample Narrative Report*

tact with the home. When narrative reports have to be translated, the school should offer this service. Community members fluent in the required language can be recruited to perform this service.

PROGRESS REPORT FORMS

Many different types of traditional and nontraditional progress report forms exist. Those discussed here are among forms found to be successful in communicating information about school performance to parents of children from diverse backgrounds.

Narrative Report Form

_____

School Name

Progress Report

Grade Level: Name of Student:

_____   _____

Date: Name of Teacher:

_____   _____

_____

Intellectual Development
Language:

Mathematical and Scientific Thinking:

Creative Development

Social and Emotional Development

Physical Development

Work Habits

General Comments (See back of page)

Figure 3–4 _Narrative Report Form_

Figures 3–1 and 3–4 show forms that have been computerized. The classroom teacher can fill out such a form very quickly, individualize it for each child, *and* print it out as a finished form. It takes time and money to develop a comprehensive outcomes-based curriculum with integrated assessments. While the initial time investment for this system was enormous, it is workable and meets the needs of the children, their families, the school, and the teachers. Included in the assessment plan is a parent handbook that explains all the components of the form as well as the curriculum, a developmental continuum describing expanding levels of performance in various content areas, the checklist shown in Figure 3–1, and a narrative report tied to district outcomes. Using a computer to update reports helps to make the task more manageable. See Chapter 11 for information about similar reporting systems.

Report forms that portray learning as a continuum can help parents from diverse backgrounds see what their children can do and how they are progressing toward desired outcomes. If the continuum indicates how children of different ages or grade levels tend to perform, parents can see how their children are performing relative to the school's expectation. The Reading Report for Continuum from Amanda Arnold School in Manhattan, Kansas, (Figure 3–5) is such a continuum.

CONCLUSION

The alternative reporting methods described in this chapter empower children from diverse backgrounds as learners, for there are no "F" or unsatisfactory grades. The skill level of each child can be accurately reported without sending negative messages. Children are compared with themselves rather than a group or entire grade level.

These strategies and alternatives to traditional report cards are effective with all students, no matter what their ethnic background. Assessment of children and communication with parents remains the classroom teacher's responsibility.

The teacher must be aware that socioeconomic background may significantly influence a child's classroom performance. A wide range of factors is involved, some as simple as whether a child is used to answering a "test-like" question. It may be more typical for children to give answers that allude to the question, or to answer in terms of their direct experiences with the topic. Other factors can be quite complex and involve deeply held family traditions and values. A child behaves differently in school if the family is supportive.

NAME _____

DATE _____

READING

Mrs. Maughmer
Grade 1

Amanda Arnold Elementary
1435 Hudson Avenue
Manhattan, KS 66502

*end of the year benchmark for first grade

(1st) ● (3rd) (4th)

1 emergent	2 beginning	3 developing	*4 maturing	5 independent
Identifies own name in print.	Beginning to perceive themselves to be readers.	Perceive themselves to be readers.	Decodes using vowels, diagraphs, blends, and letter clusters.	Extends vocabulary with new words in print.
Joins in the oral reading of stories with rhythm and rhyme.	Reads a simple book in which language patterns are repeated.	Chooses a book he/she would like to read.	Uses context to determine meaning.	Scans, skims, or reads carefully as required by the reading task.
Relies on memory for reading.	Predicts a word left out in a familiar sentence.	Uses confirmation strategies: (That word begins like my name).	Uses sentence structure to determine meaning.	Occasionally chooses challenging books.
Tells a story from pictures.	Can locate a given word in a known sentence.	Begins to self correct when reading does not make sense.	Develops further concepts of print: punctuation such as question marks and quotation marks.	Reads books with diverse genres, authors and cultures.
Is curious about print.	Is able to say another word that rhymes with a given word.	Predicts what may happen next.	Reads known and predictable books with growing confidence.	After initial reading, confidently reads a story to others with appropriate expression.
Recognizes and names the letters of the alphabet.	Uses picture clues to determine meaning.	Rereads to make sense of the text.	Chooses books for personal reading at appropriate reading level.	Uses self correction skills.
Understands the concepts of print: left to right direction, format of a book, the notion that print rather than pictures tells the story.	Can identify title on the cover of a book.	Can retell a story in sequence.	Is confident and excited when talking about a book.	Can respectfully critique literature and drama.
Identifies a letter, word, sentence, line, and space.	Begins to recognize sight words.	Has a store of sight words while reading.	Can summarize and retell a story.	Understands the interdependence of reading and writing.
Some awareness of title, author, and illustrator.	Maintains independent reading for about five minutes.	Sometimes finger points while reading.	Maintain independent reading for fifteen minutes.	Interprets and responds in written form and verbally to literature.
		Maintains independent reading for about ten minutes.		Reads and understands directions.
		Identifies title, author, illustrator and copyright date.		Maintains reading for fifteen minutes or longer.

December, 1993 **DRAFT COPY**

Figure 3–5 *Reading Report Continuum*

Some families help their children with everything connected with school: how to talk, how to answer the teacher, how to be quiet in line. Other families do not help their children with these things. It is not part of their awareness and traditions (McAfee & Leong 1994).

Regardless of which type of alternative report a teacher chooses, its success will be rooted in curriculum and assessment practices. Especially for children from diverse backgrounds and learning styles, assessment should be ongoing, and conducted by the classroom teacher rather than an outside expert (Grace & Shores 1991).

Shedlin (1988) suggests that the reporting system should be viewed as connected to teaching and learning. If it is valuable for the parents as well as the teacher, it must be considered a part of rather than an "add-on" feature of the educational program.

REFERENCES

Albemarle County Schools. 1990a. *Almost All About Narrative Reports.* Unpublished report by early childhood steering committee, Albemarle County Schools, Charlottesville, VA.

———. 1990b. *Guidelines for Writing Narrative Reports to Parents.* Unpublished report, Albemarle County Schools, Charlottesville, VA.

Bredekamp, S., ed. 1987. *Developmentally Appropriate Practice in Early Childhood Programs Serving Children from Birth Through Age 8.* Expanded edition. Washington, DC: NAEYC.

Conklin, N. & M. Lauri. 1983. *A Host of Tongues—Language Communities in the United States.* New York, NY: Free Press.

Ediger, M. 1982. *Teachers, parents and the schools.* ERIC Document Reproduction Service No. ED 254 328.

Fournier, J., B. Landsowne, Z. Pasternes, P. Steen, & S. Hudelson. 1994. "Learning With, About, and From Children: Life in a Bilingual Second Grade." In *Ways of Assessing Children and Curriculum,* ed. C. Genishi. New York, NY: Teachers College Press.

Freeman, E. & J. Hatch. 1989. "What Schools Expect Young Children to Know and Do: An Analysis of Kindergarten." *The Elementary School Journal* 89 (5):395–405.

Grace, C., & E. Shores. 1991. *The Portfolio and Its Use: Developmentally Appropriate Assessment of Young Children.* Little Rock, AR: Southern Association on Children Under Six.

Gullo, D. 1994. *Understanding Assessment and Evaluation in Early Childhood Education.* New York, NY: Teachers College Press.

Hall, K. 1989. *Determining the success of narrative report cards.* ERIC Document Reproduction Service No. ED 334 015.

Horm-Wingerd, D. 1992. "Reporting Children's Development, The Narrative Report." *Dimensions of Early Childhood* 21 (1):11–16.

Lee, F. 1992. "Alternative assessment." *Childhood Education* 69 (2):72–73.

McAfee, O. & D. Leong. 1994. *Assessing and Guiding Young Children's Development and Learning.* Boston, MA: Allyn and Bacon.

Mounts, D. 1986. *The Bi-National Migrant Child. A Research Project.* San Diego, CA: San Diego County.

Pierson, C., & S. Beck. 1987. "Performance Assessment: The Realities That Will Influence the Rewards." *Childhood Education* 70 (1):29–32.

Shedlin, A. 1988. "How about a national report card month?" *Principal* 67 (5):34.

Stiggins, R. & N. Bridgeford. 1986. In *Performance Assessment,* ed. R. A. Beck, 469–492. Baltimore, MD: The Johns Hopkins University Press.

OTHER RESOURCES

The following books and articles provide practical guidelines and management suggestions for beginning and maintaining an alternative assessment system.

Genshi, C., ed. 1994. *Ways of Assessing Children and Curriculum.* New York, NY: Teachers College Press.

Gullo, D. 1994. *Understanding Assessment and Evaluation in Early Childhood Education.* New York, NY: Teachers College Press.

McAfee, O. & D. Leong. 1994. *Assessing and Guiding Young Children's Development and Learning.* Boston, MA: Allyn and Bacon.

Section Two

A PROCESS
FOR CHANGE

Chapter 4
First Steps: Redesigning Elementary Report Cards

GLENNIE BUCKLEY

A district's decision to redesign its method of reporting student progress to parents is a much more complex matter than might be apparent to those who see only the finished product. Redesigning a report card is a *process* that must address many more issues than simply sending a report home to parents. Many questions must be answered as the redesign process unfolds. Several of those questions are discussed in this chapter:

- What is the underlying philosophy that will drive the report design?
- Will the reporting system be simply a card or will it entail a broader system of reporting?
- What does the school want families to know regarding student work and progress?
- What do families want to know about their student's work and progress in school?
- What do students need to know about their work and progress in school?
- Against what standard will the report card reflect an individual student's growth and development?
- Will the report compare students in the class or describe each student's accomplishments?
- Who will be involved in the redesign process?
- How does the process work?

- How will the report be introduced to the community?
- When and how will the report be shared with students and parents?
- What will the finished product look like?
- Will the process and product truly reflect the message the district wants to send?
- What avenues are available for input and further revision?

The following discussion of these questions assumes that the district initiating report card redesign is committed to school reform and change, and is willing to provide the support necessary to facilitate that process. The necessary support includes the following elements:

- time for developing the report card
- a facilitator, such as a central office curriculum specialist or supervisor (Pajak 1989), a director of education, or an outside consultant in districts that do not have central office staff to provide facilitative services
- staff development for both the committee members and the general teaching staff
- information that is disseminated internally and externally to the public, particularly parents, and that publicly supports the project
- secretarial staff to produce the formatted copy
- a reliable printing department or outside company that will produce the final document
- a budget that can support the project over an extended period of time and address contingencies

What is the underlying philosophy that will drive the report design?

The need for a new report card or reporting system is usually based on the need to change the way in which families are informed about the work their students are doing in school. For example, districts that embrace an integrated learning philosophy and encourage innovative, student-centered approaches to teaching may have teachers who become frustrated trying to report student progress on an outdated "grade card." Teachers find they cannot fit square pegs into round holes. It is at this point that they usually begin to call for report card reform. The district that answers that call must lay a foundation to ensure the development of a report card or reporting system that delivers what it promises: a clear picture of student progress.

Certain assumptions are inherent in this view and are key to the redesigning process. First, based on practices recommended by educational researchers and often required by both state and federal programs, a district should have in place a formal mission statement that makes public the

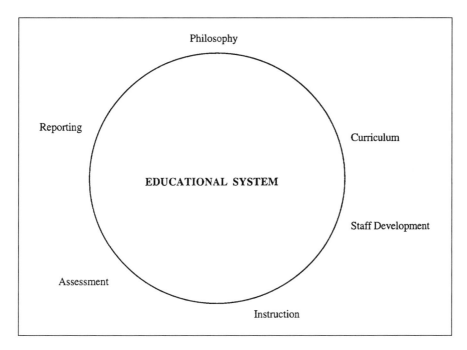

Figure 4–1 *Reporting System as Part of the Educational Cycle*

schools' mission. Second, a district should have developed a curriculum process that includes learning outcomes, objectives, and benchmarks that reflect the values of the district and that clearly state performance expectations. This curriculum process, which may take years to develop, provides the framework for the new reporting system. A mismatch among curriculum, instructional practices, and reporting procedures is often the impetus for developing a new reporting system. The reporting system should be an intricate part of the educational cycle (see Figure 4–1).

The reporting system is the primary means by which families learn not only *how* the school measures student learning but *what* the student is learning. These two facets of the reporting issue underscore the critical nature of the report and the need to be sure the message is clearly understood by all.

Will the "report" be simply a card or will it entail a broader system of reporting?

The district must decide how comprehensive to make the method of reporting. The important thing here is that teachers and parents understand the purpose and nature of appropriate assessment. The report may be a card that contains a checklist of skills, objectives, benchmarks, or outcomes in various subject areas or combinations of subject areas. The card might require teachers' descriptions of student work and involvement in learning. A reporting *system*, on the other hand, could include a portfolio assessment and/or conferences that might include teacher, parent, *and* student. Each aspect of the reporting system requires serious consideration and planning to ensure that the parts of the system support and complement one another.

What does the school want families to know about?

What to include in the report requires several major decisions that are directly related to the district's mission and outcome statements. The key cognitive/affective elements of the school's curriculum should be reflected in the reporting system. The degree of detail to be included in the report is another decision. Whatever other decisions are made, there must be a clear and direct relationship between the district's curriculum as described in curriculum guides or syllabi and the report card. The report should say something meaningful and not be simply "pseudo-communication" that leaves everyone less informed than they realize.

What do families want to know about their student's work in school?

This important but often ignored question involves two elements: meeting the expectations of families regarding the reporting system and having the opportunity to mold family expectations based on research, sound pedagogy, rich data, and appropriate assessment tools. The vast majority of families care deeply about their children's education and want them to do well in school. Generally, families want to know how their children are "doing" in the basic subjects, especially reading, language arts (including spelling), and mathematics. They want to know if their children are applying themselves, if they are "behaving" well, and if they are getting along well with others. Families are interested in the "basics" as they have come to know and understand them through personal school experiences. Beyond that, however, families may have a variety of issues that are related to school reports. Sometimes families want to know how well their children are doing compared with other students in the class. They may want to know specifics about how a particular grade was determined. They may compare one teacher's grading system with another's system. Some families want to know if their child is "gifted" or "slow."

The report card is one way families expect to get answers to these and other personal questions they have regarding their children's work in school. All too often the report card is seen not only as a report of the child's school *work* but of the child's or family's *worth.*

What do students need to know about their work?

For children, the report card traditionally has been an evaluation of their schoolwork and learning by the teacher. Historically, they have had neither a voice in what is studied and learned nor a part in determining the degree to which learning took place. Today that is changing. More and more schools are inviting students of all ages to help determine what they want and need to learn, to evaluate personal learning, and to set the course for future studies. If the reporting system is to mirror what is happening in our changing classrooms, the inclusion of students in the process would seem to be a valid consideration. Portfolios, in conjunction with teacher-parent-student conferences, are an ideal way to include students in the process. In addition, outcomes and objectives that are clearly stated in a developmentally appropriate manner can be understood by the youngest students. Therefore, there is no part of a comprehensive reporting system that should leave out the student. Students should know what is expected of them and have a voice in determining what they should expect of themselves. Then they should be coached in self-evaluation and encouraged to monitor their progress and assess their strengths and weaknesses appropriate to their age and development.

Against what standard will the report card reflect an individual student's growth and development?

The standards against which a student's progress will be measured involve delicate and extremely complex choices with the potential for both positive and negative effects. On the one hand, as educators and lay persons, we encourage students to do their best and to make strides that reflect our view of personal growth and our desire that they make continuous progress. On the other hand, we hold certain expectations regarding content to be taught, levels of learning, and the time in which the learning should take place. The problem begins there. What content should be taught and learned? What levels of learning should be expected at what ages and to what degree? Each district must answer for itself based on current educational trends, learning theory, research findings, and community expectations. The question of content demands that all parties be well informed about what content, including skills, is critical in today's world and for the future in which students will function as adults. The issues of standards and time require an understanding of how learning occurs. The fact that students learn differently and at different rates does not mean we must sacrifice high expectations, but it may require that we use a different lens through which to view progress and the attainment of outcomes. Parent and staff development and open communication among all concerned are essential to understanding these critical issues.

Will the report card compare students in the class or describe each student's accomplishments?

Report cards have traditionally been viewed as "grade" cards. On a traditional grade card, students receive a letter grade such as A (excellent), B (good), C (average), D (not up to grade), or F (failure). The method of determining and justifying a grade has often involved a point system. For instance, a report card grade in spelling is often determined by how well a student performs on weekly spelling tests. If twenty-five words are given on the test, a student who spells all the words correctly or misspells only one word receives an A. Misspelling two words might earn an A−, three a B, four a B−, and so forth.

A major problem with this grading method is that it represents a singular view of a student's work, a weekly test. In essence, the student's quarterly spelling grade, which is assumed to represent the student's spelling proficiency, is determined by eight or nine tests. No consideration is given regarding the level at which the student began, daily spelling habits in written work, or the kinds of words the student is attempting to spell.

In other subject areas, grading is done by percentages: the percentage of right answers compared to the percentage of wrong answers. While this sounds "objective," it raises the ultimate question, "A percentage of *what*?" If the percentages are based on inconsequential content, poor assessments, or unreasonable time constraints, the numbers are meaningless and often dangerous (they delude us into thinking there is meaning where there is none). Choices of content and assessment and the allocation of time to learn are subjective decisions based on belief systems. The belief system that undergirds the reporting system must be clearly understood and preferably agreed upon by those preparing and those receiving the report.

When redesigning a report card, a district must consider the contexts in which learning is being reported. Is the progress of a beginning reader being reported with regard to how the student reads familiar or unfamiliar text? Is the intermediate student's written work being evaluated on its content and organization and choice of words or on the number of mechanical errors found or lacking? Is the written work a first draft or final draft? How many drafts did the student write before she was satisfied? Has the student made steady growth or reached a plateau? Has the student not yet achieved the outcome?

Perhaps the most serious problem with the grading method is that it assigns an arbitrary grade to a student's work that is somehow equated with a "truth" about the full accomplishments of that student. In fact, it is grounded in little and often inappropriate evidence.

To emphasize that learning is a never-ending, multifaceted process, the district might consider referring to the report card as a progress report.

Such terminology supports the idea that learning is an active process rather than a static product.

Who will be involved in the redesign process?

Once the decision to redesign has been made, the redesigners must be selected. Determination of who should be involved depends in large part on the philosophy and the governance structure of the district.

The importance of including representatives from all constituencies in the district cannot be overemphasized, especially when the new reporting method is expected to be a drastic change. Internal constituencies include representative central office administrators, such as directors of elementary and secondary education and curriculum and instruction staff; building principals; classroom teachers; special education teachers; and other support staff, such as Chapter 1, remedial reading, and counselors. The key external constituency is parents. However, recognizing that districts include high numbers of households without children, some districts might find it valuable to include one or two residents who do not have children in school as a means of gaining more general support for the district's mission and future district initiatives.

No matter who is finally selected for the committee, everyone in the district should know that a new progress report is being designed and that the finished product will be brought to the entire community when it is completed.

How does the process work?

Once the committee members have been selected, the real work begins (see Figure 4–2). The larger committee or task force should meet to brainstorm key issues such as those presented here. Many different models of organizing groups are appropriate. Whichever model is selected, the facilitator should keep track of the issues and suggestions on large sheets of paper. All initial contributions should be accepted. As the process becomes redundant, the facilitator should lead the group to the next step of clustering ideas and eliminating redundancies and irrelevant ideas.

At some point the group might find it helpful to subdivide according to grade levels, whether the district uses a multi- or single-age grouping model. Each small group should then work toward defining and applying the larger group's directions in a manner appropriate for the level on which they are working. It is imperative that the various groups continually "touch base" if the reporting model is to be articulated in a clear and appropriate manner through all the grade-level outcomes. The subcommittees may find that different formats are appropriate for different grade levels as curricular emphases and instructional models change to suit the

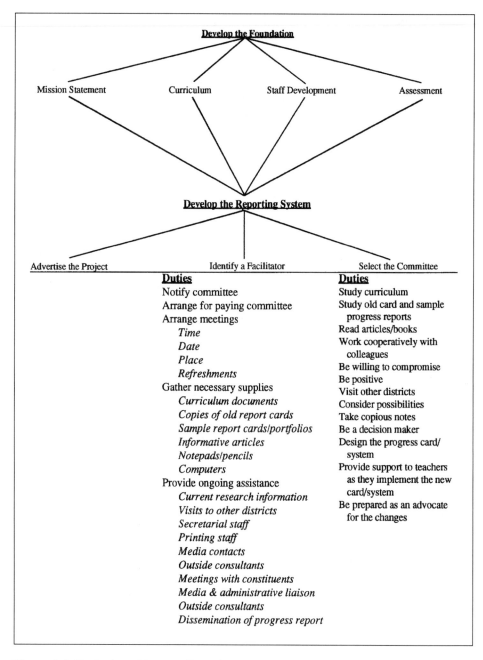

Figure 4–2 *Designing a Progress Report*

developmental needs of students. The point to remember is that the different grade-level formats of the reporting system should work in concert just as the curriculum and instructional components should.

Because of the many details to be considered, the process should not be hurried. The committee may take many weeks and even months to design an initial draft. Once the first draft is written, other district and community representatives should be invited to participate in considering the product. At this time, adjustments may be needed and compromises required. No reporting model will suit everyone's needs and wants exactly. The number of compromises will, to some degree, reflect how much the community is in agreement on the critical issues. This fact punctuates the need to lay an appropriate foundation before attempting to redesign. To ignore divergent views is to flirt with frustration and perhaps failure.

If the committee decides to redesign more than a progress report *card*, decisions must be made to integrate other facets of the reporting system. For instance, if the district already has a portfolio model, the committee must address how this will mesh with the new progress report. If no portfolio has been used, the committee may have to develop a portfolio model. A consultant can be valuable in the portfolio design. Portfolios have been the center of much research recently, yet they are not fully understood or accepted by professional educators and lay persons. Interestingly, some districts have abandoned progress cards and use *only* a portfolio system.

A major decision of the committee will involve the terminology to be used to report student progress. Will students receive a letter grade or a plus or minus mark to indicate satisfactory and unsatisfactory work? The committee should base its decision on current learning theory and appropriate pedagogy, abandon inappropriate traditional approaches (some aspects of the traditional system might be appropriate), and select positive descriptors that speak to the specific progress the student is making.

How will the report be introduced to the community?

Once the report has been designed, decisions must be made about how to introduce it to the community. Those who have guided the report from its inception may be so close to their product that they forget that it will mean dramatic changes for the faculty and community members who were not part of the design process.

Districts can use a variety of approaches to introduce the new progress report. Brochures describing the philosophy behind the report can be distributed to teachers and families. Information about committee members should be disseminated that highlights the breadth of representation from across the district and the amount of study that went into the report's design. Video demonstrations on how to complete the new progress report and how to share the information with parents and students can be an important source of support for both teachers and those with whom they will be sharing the new report. One district invited a parent to participate with a teacher in making an informational video for parents. The video was rated the best of all the district's efforts to communicate its new progress report. In larger districts, where it is not possible for all staff members to attend the same presentations, principals and at least one key teacher in each building should be given special training to help building staff and parents understand and support the new report. This principal/teacher team can later make presentations to other staff and to the parent organization.

The local newspaper can be an important source of support or criticism. Cultivating the newspaper's support should begin long before the reporting system is an issue. Informing the local education writer or a key editor about the purpose of the new report will not only help with the report but also with the larger issue of school reform. While the paper may honestly and appropriately question and critique, with proper groundwork a district can avoid a negative response that could kill the project.

The superintendent should play a key role in smoothing the way for acceptance of the new progress report. The superintendent should prepare the board of education by relating the project to changes instituted earlier in the district and supported by the board. Board members must be informed and have an opportunity to see how this innovation fits into the broad picture of school reform in the district. Because they are the representatives of the community, legally charged with overseeing the district's educational programs, board members' support is critical to the success of any change in the district.

When and how will the report be shared with students and parents?

The initial distribution of progress reports will depend in large part on the original purpose for redesigning the reporting model. Some districts choose to work through one school staffed by teachers and an administrator who are eager to be part of redesign and implementation in a pilot study. Other districts may begin working on the changes at a particular grade level. Still others will decide to bite the bullet and implement the program across the entire district.

Progress reports can be distributed at conferences one or more times during the year and sent home with students at other times. Some districts mail reports to families. Conferences may or may not include the student. Students may be asked to demonstrate progress by showing the parents their work in a portfolio and/or by reviewing with them the individual items on the report. Some teachers have students and parents help determine the student's goals for the next reporting period in an interactive conference. Such collaboration encourages productive communication among all parties.

What will the finished product look like?

The physical appearance of the report is an important consideration. A comprehensive report may require several pages or an oversized page. How many copies are needed for distribution and filing? Multi-copy paper is often used but the problem of clear copies arises if the district requires too many copies. Will the report be part of or separate from the portfolio? Will an envelope be needed? How does the product integrate with the students' permanent records? Will it fit in the permanent record folder? Will there be a paper copy or will the report be computer generated? Simple decisions such as where on the report the information related to affective behaviors can be found reveals much about what the district believes is important. When one district designed a new progress report, teachers were emphatic that the first objectives on the report would relate to behaviors. That decision was based on their belief that without the appropriate attitude and behavior, students would not and could not become actively engaged in their own learning.

Will the process and product truly reflect the message the district wants to send?

Student progress serves as a mirror reflecting the belief system that supports the district's educational philosophy and programs. An inclusive process, involving a healthy cross section of the entire community, sends the message that the district values everyone's contributions and provides a clear picture of what the district truly believes is important for students, teachers, and the community.

A well-crafted and carefully designed progress report provides an undistorted picture of how a student is progressing along the path identified in the district's mission statement and outlined in its outcomes and objectives. The district that involves its constituents, encourages well-grounded innovation, and supports positive change gives real meaning to the word *reform.*

What avenues are available for further revision?

As the district implements the new progress report, those who did not serve on the primary committee may have valid suggestions for improvements. The district must be flexible and be able to make changes in both the process and product.

Finally, because another truth is that change is certain, the district should build in a formal revision process and make sure the community is aware that the latest innovation will grow old as the others before it. The reporting system should be viewed as an ongoing process that is never really completed.

A final word of caution: neither the committee nor the district should delude itself into believing that the redesign process will be easy. Careful planning and attention to the details noted in this chapter will help. But many issues not presented here may emerge as critical in a given district. Prepare for success but be willing to accept setbacks without feeling the "agony of defeat." No matter how carefully the process is outlined and how much work is put into redesigning the progress report, resistance to change seems deeply ingrained in the human psyche and is clearly very difficult to overcome. The importance of open communication, staff development, and the continual nurturing of the individuals being asked to change cannot be overestimated. A progress report is as much a report of a district's progress as it is of a student's.

Chapter 5
Establishing Performance Standards

JANE ANDERSON AND MARCETA REILLY

L etting go of traditional grading systems can be difficult and even
frightening. Letter grades have been in place for so long, people feel
comfortable defining student progress in terms everyone understands. Everyone thinks they can recognize "A" work, or can tell when a
student shows "C," or average, ability. Unfortunately, this statement could
not be farther from the truth. One teacher's standards for an A can be very
different from another's. When using a 100-point scale, the cutoff for an A
could be a 94, or a 92, or a 90, all within the same school or even the same
grade level. These cutoffs are determined by teachers and their expectations rather than a defined set of standards.

When making a transition from a graded to a nongraded system, people
are concerned about recognizing and reporting student progress compared
to some type of standard. The question is often asked, "How will I know
the progress students are making without using a numeric score?"

Rubrics are a tool that allows us to compare student progress to a set of
defined standards related to specific outcomes. The standards have been
identified, discussed, and agreed upon by a group knowledgeable of developmentally appropriate practices. The rubric is used as a scoring guide to
judge a student's product or process. The level of performance is clearly
defined and easily compared to other levels of performance.

USING RUBRICS

In the world of performance tasks usually there is no single correct answer but rather, a variety of ways to successfully complete the tasks. Rubrics are one vehicle that can be used to guide human judgment of a performance task. Rubrics are used for the assessment of complex behaviors.

The first charge of using rubrics is to confine the task to four or five observable behaviors that will show that learning has occurred. Confine the rubric to specific behaviors and do not try to describe a global outcome. For example, a global outcome that needs many descriptors could be "uses complex thinking skills," while a more specific, observable behavior may be "uses classification to organize categories," which can be more easily defined.

The standards and indicators must be clearly and succinctly described. The rubric provides the students and parents with information about what the student will know and do. The rubric also promotes learning by offering clear targets for students. The elements of the rubric must be discussed with the students for their understanding and to promote self-assessment. When students understand the rubric, most will begin taking steps toward control of their learning and away from teacher-imposed "decision-making."

Using rubrics should be a dynamic process. Revision is necessary to create the most effective product. Students may be asked about the rubric's effectiveness and how it affected their learning. Teachers need to be aware of patterns or trends observed in students' performance. Only after several uses and changes does a rubric contain the robustness necessary to capture the essence of the desired performance.

ELEMENTS OF RUBRIC

Outcomes

The outcome is the statement of the product or activity that is to be completed. It should be broad, and should clearly define a significant knowledge, skill, or behavior. A sample outcome might be to demonstrate knowledge about the history and geography of the state by planning a vacation within the state with time and budget limitations.

Standards

Standards are the major elements, categories, or criteria that define the outcome. Standards explain to the rater (and student) what major components need to be present to perform the outcome. One standard for the vacation project could be to include data about a historical park, museum, lake, and counties in various regions of the state.

Indicators

Indicators identify what the student work looks like at each level of quality. Types of indicators for the vacation project might be the development of a data base about each region of the state, or production of a brochure about each region. The product must be defined with enough specificity so that the teacher and student can agree on the presence or absence of the quality criteria.

Levels of Quality

Levels of quality are the degree to which the student meets the standards. Examples of quality levels include "highly acceptable," "acceptable," and "not acceptable." Other levels of quality could be based on points, such as 5, 3, and 1 in the six-trait writing model (Spandel & Stiggins 1990). Decisions must be made about what levels of quality need to be demonstrated. It could be acceptable to have only "mastered" and "not mastered." Quality levels are the decision of the teacher, based on the tasks and skills to be demonstrated.

While struggling to develop useful rubrics, keep some basic ideas in mind. Focus rubrics on the *presence* of behaviors rather than the *absence* of behaviors. For example, an indicator that states "uses a twelve-inch voice" is preferable to one stating "no loud talking" when defining behaviors for cooperative groups.

Rubrics are not useful to define specific knowledge that can be easily assessed by a multiple-choice or criterion-reference test.

As indicators are developed, teachers should consider such things as accuracy, clarity, thoroughness, consistency of use, frequency of use, and timeliness.

- Accuracy Statements: Uses algorithms correctly. Capitals and periods are used in sentences.
- Clarity Statements: Describes steps of an experiment in sequence. The meaning of the passage is clear to the reader.
- Thoroughness Statements: All the steps are included. The writer includes four statements to support the main idea of the paragraph.

Math Rubrics for Assessing K-6 Outcomes
Seaman School District

Outcome: Students communicate an understanding of math concretely, verbally, and in writing.

Standard	High Quality	Acceptable Quality	Unacceptable Quality
•Computes accurately.	•Answers are consistently accurate	•High frequency of accuracy.	•High frequency of errors.
•Applies basic math facts appropriately.	•Uses basic math facts within a variety of situations.	•Uses basic math facts within most situations.	•Has difficulty using basic math facts.
•Recognizes, describes, and creates number patterns and sequence.	•Transfers recognition of patterns and sequences to situations beyond the math curriculum.	•Recognizes patterns and sequences which have been taught.	•Recognizes patterns and sequences with much assistance.
	•Describes number patterns and sequences in great detail.	•Describes number patterns and sequences with some detail.	•Describes number patterns and sequences with prompting.
	•Creates original number patterns and sequences independently.	•Creates number patterns and sequences with some modeling.	•Rarely creates number patterns and sequences.
•Explains number concepts in own words.	•Expresses understanding of number concepts.	•Expresses understanding of number concepts most of the time.	•Cannot express an understanding of number concepts.

Figure 5–1 *Math Rubrics for Assessing K-6 Outcomes*

- Consistency and Frequency Statements: The student usually completes tasks by the deadline. The student seldom interrupts other students during discussions.
- Timeliness Statements: Meets the deadline. Uses class time to complete the assignments.

This list is meant not to be exhaustive but to provide beginning points for considering criteria statements, for a variety of tasks.

BASIC RUBRIC FORMATS

A rubric is usually written as a grid with the outcome statement clearly identified, the standards down the left side of the grid, the levels of quality

Math/Science Unit
Investigating With Fractions
Sixth Grade

Outcome: Students gather and use mathematical data.

Standard	Level 4	Level 3	Level 2	Level 1
•Journal entry.	•Records a complete, accurate journal entry, describes data collection.	•Records a mostly complete, accurate journal entry describing data collection.	•Records a journal entry, but the entry is either not complete or not accurate.	•Records few facts or no journal entries; needs to start again.
•Data calculation.	•Calculates data with complete accuracy. All fractions are reduced to least common denomination.	•Calculates data accurately, most fractions are reduced to least common denominator.	•Calculates data with some accuracy, but several calculations are inaccurate and shows an incomplete knowledge of process needed; may reduce fractions incorrectly or not at all.	•Calculates data incorrectly or not at all; needs one-to-one support to reduce fractions.
•Data display.	•Shows correctly labeled data.	•Shows mostly correct labels on data.	•Shows some correctly labeled data.	•Shows no labeling of data, or labels incorrectly.
•Data reporting.	•Presents an oral report about completed project using correct mathematical terms.	•Presents an oral report completed project using some mathematical terms.	•Presents an oral report about an incomplete or inaccurate project with little or no use of correct mathematical terms.	•Does not present an oral report without individualized help.

Figure 5–2 *Math/Science Unit*

across the top, and the indicators aligned with the standard and quality levels across the page.

Figure 5–1 is an example of a three-level rubric. All students are expected to meet the acceptable level. The standards clearly describe student work rated at each level and identify for students what the teacher's expectations are. A three-level rubric is very appropriate for assessing complex learning behaviors.

A three-level rubric could also have numeric rating levels of 3-2-1 or 5-3-1. The middle level should be written as the level for all students to attain, and the distinction between levels should be clearly observable to whomever is using the rubrics.

Figure 5–2 is an example of a four-level rubric. Level 3 is the level for all students to meet. Levels 1 and 2 define in more detail than the previous example where behaviors show progress toward meeting the "acceptable" level. A four-level rubric is most appropriate when the "acceptable" level is challenging and the students need to see that they are making progress even if they have not yet reached the "acceptable" level.

Figure 5–3 is an example of a checklist rubric. All students are expected to meet the standard, which is easily observed as present or not. This kind of rubric is most appropriate for developmental scales and checklists, when the knowledge or skills being assessed are from a closed domain or are discrete: names letters of the alphabet, uses algorithms correctly, shares examples or product with the class.

DEVELOPMENT OF RUBRICS

Development of rubrics can be an individual or group process. The most useful and powerful rubrics are usually developed by groups, which can be any size from one to over one hundred people. The process is the same with any group, but is more time-consuming with larger groups.

The first step is to agree on the outcome statement. This statement is usually written by the facilitator but can be written by the group. Examples may be:

- The student works cooperatively within a group to complete a task.
- The student plans a birthday dinner for a family member, incorporating the food pyramid.

The second step in the process of rubric development is to ask individuals to think about what behaviors they observe in students who have met the outcome. These ideas can either be broad general categories or specific behaviors. Members then share their ideas in small groups and summarize them in one or two words, which are written in large letters on a description card. One card is used for each behavior. Small groups are then asked to share these descriptors with the larger group as they are taped to a large display area. As the descriptors are discussed, the group begins to cluster

Kansas Performance Assessment Committee Evaluation Rubric

Outcome: Teachers develop and use performance assessment.

Standard	Possible Indicators	Has Met Standard	In Process
•Teachers use assessments to determine whether students have achieved instructional outcomes.	•Design assessments prior to initial instruction. •Explicitly align assessments with instructional outcomes. •Reteach based on information gained from the performance assessments.	☐	☐
•Teachers use rubrics to assess learning tasks.	•Write assessment rubrics for specific learning tasks. •Collaborate with other teachers to develop and refine rubrics. •Communicate student progress with parents using rubrics. •Have students self-evaluate using rubrics. •Have students use reflection as part rubric evaluation.	☐	☐
•Teachers share examples of products with teachers and refine based on feedback.	•Present examples of products to peers. •Review examples of peers' products and offers suggestions. •Maintain portfolios of performance assessment products in their developmental stages which include reflective comments. •Enter examples of products on computer network.	☐	☐

Figure 5–3 *Kansas Performance Assessment Committee*

them into similar issues or ideas. Once the clusters are defined, each cluster must be named. These cluster names become the elements or categories for the standard.

At this point the group must decide several things:

- Who is the target audience for the rubric being developed? If the rubric is for teacher use only, teacher language can be used. If the rubric is for teacher and student use, the language used must be student-friendly.

• What levels of quality (or scoring scale) make sense for the outcome and standards that have been developed? Should the rubric scoring be a checklist or a three- or four-point scale?

Once these decisions are made, the rubric itself can be written. Using the elements or categories of the standard that were developed in the previous activity, the group begins to put into writing observable student behaviors that describe each level of quality for each element or category of the standard. These are the indicators of the outcome and standards, and clearly explain what the outcome looks like when students reach it. The group develops a common understanding of the desired outcome as it works to reach consensus on the descriptions and noteworthy behaviors, and gain agreement on vocabulary, definitions, and terms. Each person begins to see that the development of rubrics using a group consensus process is more comprehensive than when rubrics are individually developed.

After development of a rubric, individual teachers can plan instructional activities that include each of the standards. After completing the culminating activity or project and using the rubric in describing student work, teachers make necessary refinements to improve the rubric's usefulness.

Rubrics can be developed to assess individual students' behaviors, assess groups of students, assess teacher behaviors, provide proof that staff development initiatives have been implemented, and even to assess changes of an entire organization.

The most obvious advantage of developing a rubric using input from several participants is the completeness of the standards and richness of the indicators. As group members discuss the observable behaviors, each adds her definitions, understandings, and nuances. It is through the group discussions and group consensus that rubrics evolve into valuable assessment tools. Validity of group-developed rubrics is usually much better than that of individually developed rubrics.

Development by a group can also reveal the hidden curriculum. Student performance is sometimes assessed using qualities that are unrelated to the learning. Examples of factors commonly used are attendance, neatness, compliance, and respect for teacher. Open discussions allow indicators to evolve into full descriptors of the behaviors without hidden curriculum expectations.

ISSUES AND CONCERNS RELATED TO RUBRICS

Rubrics can be a valuable tool in the assessment and reporting of student learning. Use of rubrics does require preparation. Participants must explore the issues related to changing a reporting system beforehand.

Inter-Rater Reliability

The power of a rubric is the agreement that exists about rating levels among a variety of raters. The greater the degree of agreement, the more powerful the rubric. What once was "subjective judgment" now becomes "objective" because different people rate an activity or project the same way using a well-developed rubric.

But strong inter-rater reliability does not happen automatically. Teachers need to be trained in using the rubric and understanding the descriptors. Furthermore, at the beginning of any group rating session, the ratings of individual scorers need to be recalibrated by scoring some papers together to refresh the group's understanding of the descriptors.

Using Rubrics to Assign Grades

The beauty of a rubric is that it allows teachers to assess student work without assigning grades. But sometimes grades are a political reality of a school system. When rubrics are used for grading, there should be strong agreement among the raters that meeting the criteria of a certain quality level will result in assignment of a specific grade. This kind of situation is preferable to using rubrics to assess projects and complex tasks but giving grades based solely on paper-and-pencil tests. As long as teachers rely solely on traditional formats to assign grades, basic instruction will remain traditional and teacher directed. Using rubrics to assign grades gives validity to instruction that is student centered and active.

Getting Started with Rubrics

For initial use, rubrics that assess complex activities are more successfully implemented by teachers than rubrics assessing global outcomes. Teachers need to experience how rubrics work by rating writing samples or an oral speech before making the jump to assessing "citizenship" or "appreciation of the arts."

As teachers begin using rubrics, the relationship between instruction and assessment becomes clearer to both teachers and students. Teachers begin designing instructional activities that use rubrics, and students begin to focus on achieving quality rather than pleasing teachers. However, if instruction does not eventually change to regularly include student-centered learning and performance assessment, the rubric will become just another time-consuming fad that is peripheral to what goes on in the classroom.

LIMITED RESOURCES

A recent computer search found fewer than one hundred citations concerning rubrics. Further investigation found that most of the citations related to using rubrics to describe complex elements of organizational behavior or the elements of writing. Very little information could be found about developing rubrics in curricular areas and managing the information gleaned from using rubrics. Education journals are just beginning to feature this alternative form of assessment.

There are school districts and individuals that have knowledge and experience in the development and use of rubrics. They generally have had to develop their own expertise. The first use of rubrics generally resulted in thin, superficial indicators or broad indicators with little common understanding of meanings. It was only through use and revision that the rubrics became useful assessment tools.

There are too few good examples to use as models. We are just beginning to amass information about rubrics and see it published. Fortunately, this problem encourages us to rely on fellow professionals and our vast knowledge of developmentally appropriate curriculum and expectations.

OTHER RESOURCES

Jorgensen, M. 1993. "The Promise of Alternative Assessment." *The School Administrator* (December):17–23.

Marzano, R., D. Pickering, & J. McTighe. 1994. *Assessing Student Outcomes.* Alexandria, VA: Association for Supervision and Curriculum Development.

Spandel, V., & R. Stiggins. 1990. *Creating Writers: Linking Assessment and Writing Instruction.* New York: Longman.

Sperling, D., & C. Mahalak. 1993. "Using Performance Assessment To Enhance Student Learning." *Journal of Staff Development* 14 (3):36–41.

Chapter 6
Helping Teachers Make the Change

BARBARA MAUGHMER

> The future is not some place we are going to, but one we are creating. The paths are not to be found, but made, and the activity of making them changes both the maker and the destination.
>
> John Schaar
> Researcher on School Change

Change is happening everywhere, including public education. The journey is difficult for all educators but especially frustrating and uncomfortable for classroom teachers. Teachers gain professional growth one day at a time and change by seeking answers to questions that directly impact the learning of students and by seizing opportunities for leadership roles.

Much emphasis has been put on changing our teaching methods and assessment techniques. Unfortunately, our reporting instruments have lagged behind these changes. Educators are beginning to realize changes are necessary, and they must seek answers about the role of report cards. The answers to these questions may be unique to different people, but the process of change is often similar.

Classroom teachers can provide lasting educational change about which others simply theorize. Talking about change is very different from taking action, which can be difficult and sometimes frustrating. However, knowledge of the change process can make that frustration easier to understand.

Michael Fullan (Fullan & Miles 1991) refers to seven propositions for successful change. These propositions can help lay a foundation for the actual decision and action to make a change.

1. Change is Learning—loaded with uncertainty.
2. Problems are our friends.
3. Change is a journey, not a blueprint.
4. Change is systemic.
5. All large-scale change is implemented locally.
6. Change requires the power to manage it.
7. Change is resource hungry.

CHANGE IS LEARNING—LOADED WITH UNCERTAINTY

Curriculum development assessment techniques and reporting methods can be powerful change agents for classroom teachers. Decisions about what is taught and how to teach it are made by teachers several times each day. However, teachers are seldom asked to reflect on their decisions. Instead they are handed textbooks and workbooks and are expected to follow the teacher's manual. They are given report cards and grading scales and are told to report progress. Effective performance of teachers is too often based on criteria such as the quietness of the classroom, completeness of lesson plans, student performance on standardized tests, and the number of passing grades given each semester.

Teachers can begin the change process by redefining the term *curriculum development*. Teachers begin by asking questions such as why retention was expected if students could not pass a criterion-referenced test, and what information was actually shared on a traditional report card.

Teachers can begin to redefine their teaching by asking five questions:

Where are my students now?
Where do I want them to go?
How do I get them there?
How do I know when they've arrived?
How will I report the evidence I have collected?

Too often young students are given a standardized pretest, neatly diagnosed into high, middle, and low groups, and taught prescribed curriculum through the use of adopted instructional materials. Students are expected to learn the material by working independently on seatwork, participating in round-robin reading during a fifteen-minute, teacher-directed reading group, and listening to the teacher talk about the correct way to read, write, explore, and compute. Students are evaluated by averaging the scores in a grade book that have been taken from their daily work sheets. This grade is then written in a box on a report card, which is taken home to parents.

Many teachers are changing their views about the way children learn. Teachers know curriculum needs to provide students with connections between school activities and lifelong learning. Outcomes, assessment, and instructional strategies need to be clearly defined and shared up front with students and parents. Lessons need to focus on lifelong learning and assessment to provide evidence that the learner outcome has been demonstrated. A student-centered classroom allows decisions and spontaneity to be generated by students and teachers and to occur within the actual teaching process. Reporting student progress should be a collaboration among teacher, student, and parents. Teachers often find that the "orderly" classroom of the past does not work in this new setting. When applying traditional curricula to a classroom that endorses decision making by students, teachers find the prescribed curriculum does not merge with their philosophical beliefs about how children learn. Fullan's proposition that "change is learning" becomes real. Teachers know what they want their students to accomplish during the school year, but they can no longer use the prescribed materials, tests, and report cards to answer those questions we ask about our students.

PROBLEMS ARE OUR FRIENDS

Strong professional beliefs are very important as teachers continue to change. These guiding beliefs become the foundation for all decisions, small or large, inside or outside the classroom, and should be clearly communicated.

Guiding beliefs should drive all professional growth. Many teachers do not understand the importance of a clear vision and how imperative it is to the change process. Schools often develop a vision statement, but it is seldom practiced by teachers. Teachers need to internalize their personal beliefs and mesh them with the school vision statement through practice, not theory. Teachers' ownership of the vision becomes obvious when they reflect on and self-assess their teaching on a regular basis. Communicating these beliefs to parents, students, other educators, and the general public often puts teachers in a defensive position. But, as Fullan says, "Problems are our friends." As teachers begin to defend what and how they teach, they gain complete ownership and see change not as a "problem" but as a "critical friend" that helps them grow professionally. A clear vision is a must if teachers are to make fundamental changes.

This vision is ultimately reflected in our reporting system. The use of letter grades and checklists reflect what we value in our classroom. Ideally, teachers will use a reporting system that matches their professional beliefs. However, having defined our beliefs, we realize a traditional report card asks us to report irrelevant or unnecessary information. This gap between our beliefs and the current report system is seen as a "problem." Realization of this problem motivates teachers to take action and realign the reporting system with their beliefs.

CHANGE IS A JOURNEY, NOT A BLUEPRINT

Effective change cannot be packaged and sold. Staff development is the journey . . . instructional and assessment strategies are the blueprint. Instructional and assessment materials, and report forms purchased or adopted without adequate staff development, often hinder rather than help the change process.

Teachers have traditionally received professional development and in-service training by attending workshops, seminars, and graduate classes. Too often this approach to staff development has provided teachers with a knowledge base for educational concepts but little time for development of ideas, practice, feedback, and reflection. Consequently, little or no impact on student learning occurred.

We have come to realize that the most effective staff development occurs when teachers have time to collaborate and reflect together. Theory and research become the basis for professional development through reading, attending conferences, and teleconferencing. By interacting with those who write the theory, teachers use professional materials to assist with ongoing changes in their classrooms.

Once the theories are grounded in a belief system, teachers often become action researchers: "Action research is designed, conducted, and implemented by teachers themselves to improve teaching in their own classrooms, sometimes becoming a staff development project in which teachers establish expertise in curriculum development and reflective teaching. Very often action research is a collaborative activity where practitioners work together to help one another design and carry out investigations in their classroom" (Johnson 1993).

Action research helps teachers make informed decisions about the outcomes they want their students to develop and about the instructional strategies needed to obtain those outcomes. When teachers view their classrooms as research laboratories, their minds are opened to view learning in a different way. They are challenged to develop multiple strategies to assess and report student growth. Change should be a journey, not a blueprint, which encourages teachers to grow professionally by seeking additional training. Workshops, seminars, and professional journals can all enhance teachers' action research.

CHANGE IS SYSTEMIC

Through practice, feedback, and reflection teachers begin to realize that everything that happens in a classroom affects others in the system. Teaching can no longer be viewed as an isolated act.

As Glennie Buckley writes in Chapter 4, all stakeholders need to be involved in change. Changing a progress report involves not only the teachers, but also the students, parents, administrators, and the community. Communication and understanding among all stakeholders is essential. Effective staff development is the core to implementing lasting changes. From this point, change ripples out and affects all aspects of this community. Effective staff development is the key to uniting stakeholders in the change process. A good staff development program should have an element of teacher choice that allows for a district focus as well as individual growth possibilities. It should provide a structure that enhances communication between teachers, administrators, professional associations, students, parents, and other "critical friends" of education. Support groups, study groups, and teacher-taught seminars are effective ways to allow choice and provide individual growth opportunities. Monthly meetings allow teachers to share classroom frustrations and celebrations, stay abreast of research, and make formal presentations in a supportive environment. Change is a slow process, and teachers gain strength by supporting one another. When this occurs, teachers begin to share excitement for change with students, parents, administrators, and other teachers in the building.

ALL LARGE-SCALE CHANGE IS IMPLEMENTED LOCALLY

Large-scale change must be clearly defined and implemented at the classroom level. Traditional governance models may interfere with the change process. Teacher empowerment must be valued by administration. Trust must be established. Principals need to visibly support teacher decision making and leadership positions through conversations with parents and other district administrators. Top-down and bottom-up change must coexist in a delicate balance. Policy can dictate large-scale change, but lasting change will only occur when teachers, students, and parents work together to understand and implement these changes. Report cards that use letter grades or percentages have been a central feature of American schools for many years. Changing attitudes about letter grades requires all stakeholders to engage in open, honest discussion. Implementing effective change at the local level becomes very complex because it must be presented in a simple, consistent, and concise manner.

CHANGE REQUIRES THE POWER TO MANAGE IT

As classroom teachers become involved in the change process, they must assume new roles and develop new skills. The change process is complex and often produces anxiety. This can be alleviated through formal and informal partnerships. Two such partnerships have been especially helpful since our building embarked on its change journey. When our school was invited to become one of six Mastery in Learning Consortium sites by the National Education Association (NEA) Center for Innovation, teachers were slow to say yes. The thought of adding "one more task" was almost overwhelming. However, by becoming part of the consortium, the staff gained much-needed support for their innovation through the NEA. The consortium provided a national perspective, access to current researchers who were also focusing on improving student learning. The Center for Innovation provided a site consultant who, in addition to being a critical friend, trained the staff in management and conflict. The NEA understood change requires the power to manage it.

Another personal example of partnership occurred when our district engaged in a strategic planning process. This process resulted in a district focus on outcomes-based education and a collaborative arrangement with a local university. Many teacher-leaders throughout the district were asked to become involved. Again, our teachers wanted to practice what they had learned about collaboration, assessment, and the change process. As a result, many undergraduate education students are gaining valuable classroom and building experiences through this partnership. Classroom teachers are creating time for collaboration by having more adults in the building to help with teaching responsibilities. We also have added another half-time teacher-leader position to coordinate this program. The coordinator deals with the teachers' frustration in trying to juggle their time to collaborate with team teachers, university students, the library media specialist, special education teachers, the art teacher, and others who help integrate instruction.

As teachers begin to ask questions about current reporting systems, they need a wide variety of resources to support their inquiry.

CHANGE IS RESOURCE HUNGRY

To provide for the individual needs of all students, a classroom teacher must have a thorough knowledge of current research along with the flexibility of choosing appropriate materials for the classroom. Results occur when the large span between research and practice is eliminated. Attendance at conferences, professional reading, and networking with colleagues are necessary to the process. Action research projects lead to new insights. This collaborative effort often results in tremendous personal and professional growth.

SUMMARY

Classroom teachers can powerfully affect change in education by leading in the following ways:

- reflecting on curriculum development
- clearly communicating expectations to all stakeholders
- selecting resources, instruction, and assessment that connects school activities with lifelong learning
- establishing a clear vision and guiding beliefs
- seeking additional training through workshops, seminars, and professional journals
- becoming involved in action research
- forming support groups, leading study groups, and teaching district seminars
- becoming a member of the district committee that focuses on curriculum revision and encouraging curriculum development as a district responsibility
- interpreting and communicating large-scale changes in common language to all stakeholders
- assuming formal and informal leadership positions
- seeking opportunities for outside support through partnerships

In our building, all of the resources described in this chapter came together to help us translate the district's exit outcomes (see Figure 6–1) into building benchmarks, were then used to inform our teaching and led to the revision of our reporting system. Lisa Biteau, in Figure 11–2, shared the way she has interpreted the outcomes for her multi-age, intermediate classroom. Figures 6–2 and 6–3 show how the outcomes were addressed in my

LEARNER OUTCOMES

Our mission is to educate each student to be a contributing citizen in a changing, diverse society.

We will know our students are contributing citizens for a changing diverse society when they are:

EFFECTIVE COMMUNICATORS, Who
> Clearly express ideas and effectively communicate with diverse audiences, through a variety of mediums, and for a variety of purposes.

SELF-DIRECTED LEARNERS, Who
> Create a positive vision for themselves and their future, set priorities and achievable goals, create options for themselves, monitor and evaluate their progress, and assume responsibility for their actions.

COMPLEX THINKERS, Who
> Identify, access, integrate, and use available resources and information to reason, make decisions, and solve complex problems in a variety of contexts, and translate issues and situations into manageable tasks that have a clear purpose.

QUALITY PRODUCERS, Who
> Create intellectual, artistic, practical, and physical products which reflect originality, high standards, and the use of advanced technologies.

COLLABORATIVE WORKERS, Who
> Use effective leadership and group skills to develop and manage interpersonal relationships within culturally and organizationally diverse settings.

COMMUNITY CONTRIBUTORS, Who
> Contribute their time, energies, and talents to improving the welfare of others and the quality of life in their diverse communities.

Figure 6–1 *Learner Outcomes*

PROGRESS TOWARD U.S.D. 383 DISTRICT OUTCOMES

I see her progressing toward the district outcomes as follows:

EFFECTIVE COMMUNICATOR
Is reading and writing with confidence. She loves to read aloud to the class. When reading she uses several good strategies including self correction and repeating to improve comprehension. She uses phonics to decode words, uses the context of the story to help clarify meaning and has good use of picture cues. She has wonderful ideas for writing and is beginning to organize and develop them on paper. She loves creative dramatics and enjoyed being the director of her play. She is a selective listener - listening when she so desires, but she never distracts others from listening.

COMPLEX THINKER
enjoys projects that demonstrate her use of higher-level thinking. She loves math and science and has no trouble describing how she derived an answer.

SELF-DIRECTED LEARNER
independently seeks information from various sources including me and her peers. She loves to learn and is participating more and more in group discussions.

QUALITY PRODUCER
selects what she wants to complete. Those projects are always finished with great care but other projects go unfinished. Her penmanship is not always neat.

COLLABORATIVE WORKER
works well cooperatively in a whole group, small group and partner setting. She enjoys taking a leadership role.

COMMUNITY CONTRIBUTOR
is a caring and thoughtful student who obeys the rules and is considerate of others. She usually keeps her desk and personal area clean.

_____   _____
Date   Signature

1993-1994
FIRST GRADE PROGRESS REPORT
fourth nine weeks

_____ has been promoted to second grade for the 1994-95 school year.

U.S.D. 383
Amanda Arnold Elementary School
1435 Hudson
Manhattan, Kansas 66502
(913) 587-2020

Barbara Maughmer
classroom teacher

PERSONAL GOALS FOR THE FOURTH
NINE WEEK PERIOD 4/4/94-6/3/94

SUMMER RECOMMENDATIONS:
Practice math facts to 20.

DEMONSTRATED THESE GOALS:
Published 6 books the second nine weeks (her goal was 5)
complete a task on time
keep desk organized
read Amelia Bedelia with fluency by the end of first grade
publish three stories using prewriting strategies
Project voice when speaking to a group
Count money using pennies, nickels, dimes and quarters

COMMENTS:
I have truly enjoyed _____ this year. We will miss your entire family at our school. Best of luck in your new home.

	Absent	Tardy
1st qtr	0	0
2nd qtr	3	0
3rd qtr	4	0
4th qtr	0	0

Primary-level progress report

Figure 6–2 *Personal Goals*

FIRST GRADE OUTCOMES

4   Demonstrates Most of the Time
3   Demonstrates Some of the time
2   Not Yet Demonstrated
*   Not evaluated at this time

EFFECTIVE COMMUNICATOR

LANGUAGE ARTS

THE CHILD WILL ..

develop a positive attitude and appreciation for literacy

use the reading process to develop reading skills*

use the writing process to develop written communication skills*

develop oral communication skills; conveys many kinds of information and ideas through discussion. uses appropriate language to solve problems.

develop spelling skills; absorbs spelling concepts; applies spelling in writing

develop listening skills;

apply correct penmanship form

use beginning library skills; uses the library on a regular basis understands the layout of a library applying library concepts

Evidence of progress can be seen in the student's portfolio.
*Refer to the performance criteria scoring guides in his/her portfolio

COMPLEX THINKER

MATHEMATICS

THROUGH THE USE OF MANIPULATIVES, THE CHILD WILL

acquire number sense in math terminology, counting, addition and subtraction, word problems, estimation, and place value*

demonstrate understanding of measurement in the areas of telling time, money, calendars, and measuring

demonstrate understanding of the use and functions of patterns and geometry

demonstrate understanding of creating and interpreting graphs

SCIENCE/HEALTH

SCIENCE PROCESS SKILLS

THROUGH THESE THE CHILD WILL FURTHER HIS/HER UNDERSTANDING OF ....

earth science (weather, rocks/soil and space)

physical science (beginning chemistry..liquids/solids and magnets)

life science (plants, animals, and ecology)

health science (human sexuality, nutrition, emotional health, safety/first aid, substance use and abuse)

QUALITY PRODUCER

TECHNOLOGY

demonstrate beginning computer skills

COMMUNITY CONTRIBUTOR

SOCIAL STUDIES

THE CHILD WILL FURTHER HIS/HER UNDERSTANDING OF....

the family

relationships with others

safe living

Kansas history, African-American history, holidays, great Americans and American symbols

geography

QUALITY PRODUCER

MUSIC

THE CHILD ....

will learn music through reading, clapping, rhythms, singing, moving, and playing instruments.

is expected to behave in accordance with the music rules which include following directions, keeping bodies to self, listening, treating others and equipment with respect, and exerting a good effort.

ART

THE CHILD WILL DEVELOP UNDERSTANDINGS AND CONCEPTS ABOUT...

line, shape, form, color, visual composition, and texture

experience the interrelatedness of art and other curricular activities

become familiar with the art medium of collage, painting, drawing, ceramics, printmaking, and paper sculpture

PHYSICAL EDUCATION

THE CHILD WILL BE EXPECTED TO..

participate to the best of their ability in various games, movement, fitness, gymnastic, and rhythmic activities

cooperate with other students in group activities

listen and follow directions

COLLABORATIVE WORKER

SOCIAL SKILLS

THE CHILD WILL....

demonstrate appropriate school behavior

develop a good self-concept

practice self-control

respect the rights of others

respect personal property and that of others

cooperate with others

SELF-DIRECTED LEARNER

WORK-STUDY SKILLS

THE CHILD WILL....

follow directions

make good use of time

work at his/her ability to produce quality work

develop self-responsibility

develop problem solving skills

develop critical thinking skills

Primary-level learning targets

Figure 6-3 *First Grade Outcomes*

primary classroom. Other teachers are at different places in the process of developing report cards for their classrooms.

I fondly remember the excitement I felt when I accepted my first teaching position. Teaching continues to provide me with that same excitement. As I reflect on my years as a classroom teacher, I realize it is not teaching that excites me. Rather, it is learning that provides the needed motivation to survive in public education today. If we want to produce lifelong teachers, we must model lifelong learning.

REFERENCES

Fullan, Michael & Matthew Miles. "Getting Reform Right: What Works and What Doesn't." *Phi Delta Kappan* 73 (10):744–752.

Johnson, Beverly. 1993. "Teacher-As-Researcher." *ERIC Digest* 92 (7).

OTHER RESOURCES

Allen, JoBeth. 1989. *Risk Makers, Risk Takers, Risk Breakers: Reducing the Risks for Young Literacy Learners.* Portsmouth, NH: Heinemann.

Bietau, L., J. Crill, & B. Maughmer. 1993. The Manhattan Assessment Project. *Student Portfolios.* Washington DC: NEA Publications.

Dismuke, Diane. 1993. "Are Report Cards Obsolete?" *NEA Today* 11 (9):12–13.

Fullan, M. 1991. *The New Meaning of Educational Change.* New York, NY: Teachers College Press.

Glickman, Carl. 1990. "Pushing School Reform to a New Edge: The Seven Ironies of School Empowerment." *Phi Delta Kappan* 72 (1):68–75.

Graves, Donald. 1981. *Writing: Teachers and Children at Work.* Portsmouth, NH: Heinemann.

Harste, Jerome. 1984. *Language Stories and Literacy Lessons.* Portsmouth, NH: Heinemann.

Holdaway, Don. 1979. *The Foundations of Literacy.* Portsmouth, NH: Heinemann.

Maughmer, B., L. Bietau, J. Crill. 1993. "Assessing a Community of Learners: Authentic Assessment in Action." *Kansas ASCD Record* 11 (2):53–64.

———. 1993. "Benefits of the Assisting Teacher." *Views, Insights and Perspectives* (October–November):6–8.

Smith, Frank. 1983. *Essays into Literacy.* Portsmouth, NH: Heinemann.

Watson, Dorothy. 1985. *Observing the Language Learner.* Urbana, IL: NCTE.

Chapter 7
A Personal Perspective

BILLIE MANDERICK

I've taught first grade for seventeen years. I began as a traditional teacher, focusing mainly during the day on basal reader reading groups, related workbook assignments, and reams of phonics and math work sheets. The work sheets were "busy work" for students who were not in the reading group that was currently reading with me. My teaching style changed little from year to year. It consisted of the same basal reader stories with controlled vocabulary, presented in the same order, faithfully read to me by students in one ability group after another, year after year, until the students and I were bored silly. Math consisted of quiet, individual computation practice on one page of the consumable math book each day, removed from any meaningful context. Near the end of the day, we would get out our science, social studies, or health books and read and discuss them together.

For this type of traditional classroom the traditional type of reporting system was fine. There was a place to mark whether students were getting their work done. (But was it their work or mine?) There was a place to mark whether or not they respected authority. (But what about respecting each other?) There was an area in the reading section entitled "Knows basic vocabulary." (How could I possibly believe that all students should or could learn all of the reader's required vocabulary during first grade?) There was an area in the spelling section called "Learns assigned words." (How could a student who could not read the words on the prescribed spelling list possibly learn to spell them?) Under social studies and science/health, there was "Participates in activities." (There were precious few meaningful activities in these areas, and the students really had no choice about whether they participated or not. They had no choice in what projects we did and could see no reason to do them other than that they were in the textbook.)

In the math section there was "Knows and uses addition facts. Knows and uses subtraction facts." (But did the students know why they were to know them, of what use they were, or even exactly what they stood for?)

Although during those first few years I did begin to have my students do some assigned writing, did begin to develop a few thematic units, and did plan related field trips, the district's philosophy remained the same, and the reporting system continued to fit. My teaching, assessment, and reporting systems were aligned. But I was burned out.

I began to change my teaching methods. As a result of reading professional books by such authors as Donald Graves and Frank Smith, talking with other teachers, and reflecting on what was really going on in my classroom, I began to give up some control and trusted my students to take responsibility for their learning. I initiated a daily writing workshop in which my students generated their own writing projects. They loved it. It was their work, not mine. They were invested in it, and few were ever off task. To make time for the workshop, I reduced my four or five reading groups to two. As the writing workshop flourished, I no longer needed the English and spelling texts, so I stopped using them. I could see and document that students were learning conventional spelling and grammar within the context of their daily writings, not to mention learning to write a good story! Since I was no longer making class assignments such as spelling tests and English pages, I had to make a change in the report card in the areas entitled "Learns assigned words" and "Learns language rules." So I simply crossed off those areas and continued only to mark the areas that asked if the student was applying skills. Since different students were learning different skills at different times, everyone was succeeding. I now felt that I was truly reporting what they knew, not what they seemed to know based on my examination of their spelling test or fill-in-the-blank English workbook exercises. Those assignments were really only evidence of memorized (often temporarily) skills and not the actual use of those skills in authentic writing.

Now I needed an area to report student writing ability. The only time that the word *writing* appeared was in the three areas listed under the category of handwriting! Yes, three areas in which to evaluate handwriting and none addressing actual writing! I began saving samples of student writing to share with parents at conference time, pointing out their students' growing abilities in content and conventions. I wanted parents to understand that even though writing was not addressed on the report card, it was important! Thus began my portfolio assessment.

Just for good measure I crossed off one area under handwriting, "Forms letters and numbers correctly." I'd never been comfortable with that one. If a student's handwriting was reasonably neat and legible, why was it so important to strictly follow the prescribed ball-and-stick method of forming letters? Adults have their own handwriting style. Why don't we allow our students this same freedom? Now I was on a roll. I felt I was making this report mine, not the district's, and I could better invest myself in filling it out.

As time and the writing workshop went on, I dropped all reading groups. Students were learning to read through their writing, through whole-group shared reading experiences, and through simply being given the daily time to spend with books of their choice. My role (and the role of the students themselves) became more of guide and facilitator when students needed the help of someone more experienced. I began to present mini-lessons on skills to individuals, small groups, and sometimes the whole class when I would see the need and the readiness. I treated the reading series as a literature set. We chose stories we all could enjoy together when they tied in with something that was being studied in other curriculum areas. Children having difficulty with decoding now were not excluded from developing other reading skills and enjoying good literature.

This new way of thinking about reading did not fit with the old report card. So now I had to cross out the area that read, "Knows basic vocabulary." The natural readers were spending time with longer books that contained varied vocabulary. The others were also working at their own levels, learning words at their own pace, as they reached a stronger understanding of the written code. No one was being set up for failure on the report card or in life! Because we were no longer doing the daily round-robin thing, I also decided to cross off "Reads well orally." I had students who were only reading familiar, predictable material, which is an important developmental stage in emergent literacy. I also had students who were reading anything and everything. How was I to define "Reads well orally"? How was I to mark it without being misleading? Cross it off! What I really needed were two new areas to evaluate: "Reads familiar material" and "Reads unfamiliar material." There is a difference, and both are important achievements. Yet there was nowhere on the card to put them.

With developmentally appropriate practices in place in the area of language arts, it was time to look at the rest of my program. What changes did I want to make to align the other curricular areas with my new philosophy? From further studies, attendance at workshops, and more reflection, I learned how to make my math program much more than just practice in computation. I provided authentic, problem-solving experiences. Students could develop their own strategies for finding solutions, then share and discuss strategies among themselves. Communication in math is one of the district math standards, but it is not addressed on the report card. I also provided more opportunities for students to explore patterns, the basis of all mathematics, as well as to explore shapes in a much more in-depth manner than before. I felt that I had to alter the areas under math on the report card that read, "Knows and uses addition/subtraction facts." I now realized that it was inappropriate to have first graders memorize facts before they had the opportunity to spend time exploring with manipulatives, within the context of authentic classroom math situations. So I revised the statement to read, "Uses addition and subtraction," then added "Understands patterns" and "Understands shapes" in the blank area at the end of the math section.

To tie in other curricular areas, I also planned learning and interest centers around the room where students could engage in hands-on activities in the areas of science and social studies, as well as math and language arts.

When I mentioned to colleagues about how I was altering the report card, many were incredulous! How could I do that? Did I get permission? Well, that depends. Permission from whom? I gave myself permission, as a professional who was trying to do the best job I knew how to do at the time. My principal was unaware of my activities, as far as I knew. I had never thought to check with him. My students' parents did not question me for I was able to explain my reasoning to them. They were not fools. They knew their students loved to learn with me, and that their students were learning. They were, for the most part, familiar with what was going on in the classroom and how their students were doing. I have for many years maintained an open-door policy, meaning that I encourage parents to join in our day whenever they wish, no appointments necessary. For many years I have also invited each parent to read a story to the class, help with an art or cooking project, or share something of interest with us. Most have taken me up on the invitation. I have encouraged them to stay afterwards, as additional experienced persons who could help the students with their literature responses or thank-you projects. In this way, parents have been able to get to know their student's classmates, teacher, and learning environment.

Throughout the school year, my students, their parents, and I were all learning and growing together. But the report card was starting to look pretty bad, with all of the crossouts and additions. I was very unhappy with the indicators "unsatisfactory," "satisfactory," and "highly satisfactory." The first gave the message to the parent and the child that the child was a failure. This message had to be damaging. I did not want to use "unsatisfactory," but I could be misleading parents if I checked "satisfactory" for an area in which a student was not yet able to perform with any competency. I had not yet learned what were to become my favorite terms: "not yet" and "emerging." My only choice was to leave those areas blank, for the students not yet achieving in that area.

The terminology on the report card was all so judgmental and ambiguous. Satisfactory work, in the opinion of this teacher, might be unsatisfactory to another teacher. In addition, such indicators seemed to say that all children should be learning the same thing at basically the same time. However, we know that, although all children go through the same stages in their development, they do not develop at the same rate or at the same time. Why must we pass an unsatisfactory judgment on a child simply because, for whatever reason, (developmental, cultural, emotional, or physical) the student is just "not getting it yet"? What was I going to do?

I was not alone in my frustration with the report card. The school district decided to design a new one (see Figure 7–1). With feedback from teachers, parents, curriculum specialists, and administrators, I worked on a committee that designed a new progress report. Our committee designed a child-sensitive, developmentally appropriate form with no "unsatisfactory" indicator. The form was aligned with the new curriculum guides, which called for a more in-depth, developmentally appropriate curriculum.

Indicators were changed from the judgemental "unsatisfactory," "satisfactory," and "highly satisfactory" to statements of facts "not yet," "emerging," "usually," and "regressing." The new indicators show an understanding of the learning process. Because a student does not yet show an understanding of a certain concept or skill does not mean the student's progress is unsatisfactory. The student is just not getting it *yet*. Although I feel the terminology is a step in the right direction, I am uncomfortable with the indicator "regressing." Progress made with any emergent skill is an up-and-down road, with variable speed and an occasional stop sign. Slow or no progress does not mean the student is regressing. In addition, if a serious problem does arise, parents should be notified immediately, in person, not on the report card later at report card time.

But overall I was pleased with the changes in the report card. Many teachers were pleased. Some others grumbled. Still others loudly protested. This new reporting system was not aligned with their still traditional ways of teaching. They had not accepted the new paradigm. Some never will. The school board also had a difficult time understanding the changes since its members did not have an understanding of the new philosophy on which the changes were based. Fortunately, the board members did not have the responsibility to make a decision about implementing the new progress report. The responsibility belonged to the director of elementary education, and she enthusiastically gave her approval. The report card was printed (enough for one year) with "working draft" at the top. Teachers were given in-service training and parents were informed of the changes. The local newspaper printed a copy of the progress report and caused quite a furor in the community with its less than adequate understanding of the reporting form and the philosophy upon which it was based. Change does

TOPEKA PUBLIC SCHOOLS, USD #501
1993-94

1st GRADE PROGRESS REPORT

	1			2				3				4			
	Not Yet	Emerging	Usually	Not Yet	Emerging	Usually	Regressing	Not Yet	Emerging	Usually	Regressing	Not Yet	Emerging	Usually	Regressing
ATTITUDES AND BEHAVIORS															
Monitors own behavior			✓			✓				✓				✓	
Takes initiative			✓			✓				✓				✓	
Uses time wisely			✓			✓				✓				✓	
Seeks help			✓			✓				✓				✓	
Demonstrates effort			✓			✓				✓				✓	
Shows respect for others			✓			✓				✓				✓	
Works cooperatively			✓			✓				✓				✓	
Interacts with peers			✓			✓				✓				✓	
Takes responsibility for materials			✓			✓				✓				✓	
Returns notes, supplies, homework			✓			✓				✓				✓	
LANGUAGE ARTS															
LISTENING															
Listens to others			✓			✓				✓				✓	
Follows oral directions			✓			✓				✓				✓	
Retells a story			✓			✓				✓				✓	
Makes predictions			✓			✓				✓				✓	
Responds to reading selections			✓			✓				✓				✓	
			✓			✓				✓				✓	
SPEAKING															
Formulates questions to get information			✓			✓				✓				✓	
Participates in class discussions			✓			✓				✓				✓	
Stays on topic in group discussions			✓			✓				✓				✓	
Shares projects with the class			✓			✓				✓				✓	
WRITING															
Uses the writing process (pre-write, compose, revise, edit, publish)			✓			✓				✓				✓	
Sees self as writer			✓			✓				✓				✓	
Chooses to write			✓			✓				✓				✓	
Uses conventions (grammar, punctuation, capitalization)	✓			✓				✓				✓			
Applies spelling skills	✓			✓				✓						✓	
Writes for various purposes			✓			✓				✓				✓	
Invests self in projects			✓			✓				✓				✓	
Writes legibly and neatly in daily work	✓					✓				✓				✓	
READING															
Participates in shared reading			✓			✓				✓				✓	
Reads familiar material			✓			✓				✓				✓	
Reads unfamiliar material	✓			✓						✓				✓	
Sees self as reader			✓			✓				✓				✓	
Chooses to spend time with books			✓			✓				✓				✓	
Uses various strategies to read unfamiliar words	✓			✓						✓				✓	
Expands vocabulary	✓					✓				✓				✓	
Develops comprehension skills			✓			✓				✓				✓	
Reads for various purposes										✓				✓	
Invests self in projects			✓			✓				✓				✓	

Figure 7–1 *First Grade Progress Report*

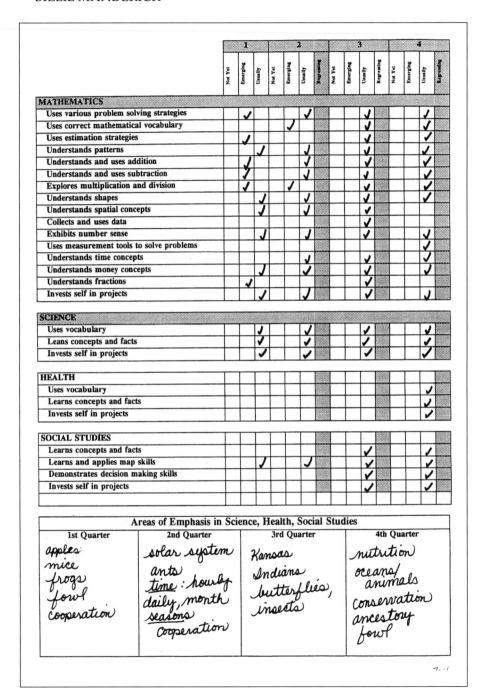

Figure 7–1 (*Continued*)

	1				2				3				4			
	Not Yet	Emerging	Usually	Progressing	Not Yet	Emerging	Usually	Progressing	Not Yet	Emerging	Usually	Progressing	Not Yet	Emerging	Usually	Progressing
ART																
Invests self in projects			✓				✓				✓				✓	
MUSIC																
Matches pitches			✓				✓				✓				✓	
Moves to steady beat			✓				✓				✓				✓	
Sings melody in tune																
Recognizes musical form																
Demonstrates appropriate behavior			✓			✓					✓				✓	
PHYSICAL EDUCATION																
Shows growth in skills		✓				✓					✓				✓	
Participates in activities		✓				✓					✓				✓	
Practices safety rules		✓				✓					✓				✓	
Uses equipment properly		✓				✓					✓				✓	
Demonstrates good sportsmanship		✓				✓					✓				✓	
Demonstrates appropriate behavior		✓					✓				✓					✓

1st Quarter Comments

David is an attentive, hard-working student. He has shown a lot of growth in his reading and writing skills.

2nd Quarter Comments

David is writing long stories with highly developed plots and mature vocabulary. He has an excellent grasp of money and clock time concepts.

3rd Quarter Comments

David is a true reader and writer. He is very creative. He is well behaved and takes initiative.

4th Quarter Comments

David is admired by his classmates for his good-nature, creativity and studious nature. Encourage him to continue his writing outside of school.

ASSIGNMENT FOR NEXT YEAR: GRADE ___2___

Figure 7–1 *(Continued)*

not come easily! Some components of education have not changed in many, many years, and every generation has difficulty seeing things done that differ from their school experiences. School traditions are almost sacred to many people.

This progress report is indeed different. A section is devoted to the four areas of language arts: reading, writing, listening, and speaking, which takes the place of the main headings of reading, spelling, and English on the old report card. Two areas to be evaluated under both reading and writing are "chooses to read/write" and "invests self in projects." These are very important life skills that have never been addressed before. How many students work only because it is required of them, to please their parents or teachers, or to get a high grade? They then promptly forget what was "learned" when the class or test is over. When students are given no choices, they make little investment in their learning. Choices encourage students to internalize their learning. Choice and investment need to be evaluated on any progress report, but they can only be evaluated when encouraged within the classroom.

"Basic vocabulary" is not mentioned under reading. Instead, we use "expands vocabulary." Growth in vocabulary shows the development of a student at any reading level. We also use "sees self as reader/writer." These areas need to be considered and reported on. The children's view of themselves directly affects their internalization of learning.

Handwriting ("writes neatly and legibly in daily work") is a single item within the writing section. This puts writing and handwriting in proper perspective.

Instead of the old "English" section, the writing section includes "uses conventions (grammar, punctuation, capitalization)." Also under writing, "applies spelling skills" replaces an entire section on spelling on the old form. Spelling is important but only within the context of authentic writing projects.

The new progress report contains a much more complete math section. Each of the national math standards is evaluated. "Memorizes facts" is not included until second grade.

The area addressing behaviors and attitudes, which replaces the old "general behavior and work habits," is now at the beginning of the form rather than the end. This change is an attempt to relate to parents the importance of these two areas. Under the heading "behaviors and attitudes," we see "respects others," not just "respecting authority," as reported on the old form. Attention is also given to whether the student interacts with peers, not just whether the student gets along with them. There is a difference. Of course, the classroom environment must allow for frequent, daily interaction for these areas to be fairly evaluated. Having rows of quietly working, robotic students most or all of the day is not developmentally appropriate. It is not how children best learn. Nor adults!

On the new form, teachers have an entire section to write positive, constructive comments each quarter. The size of this section is a big improvement over the skimpy section on the old form, which had only enough space for one quarter's comments.

The new progress report is child-sensitive, developmentally appropriate, and aligned with the curriculum. The report does tell the parents much more about their child's learning. It does do a much better job of reflecting my personal teaching philosophy. I expected to love it. I don't.

After using the progress report the first year, I found some problems. Simply by including certain items to be evaluated, the district sends the message to parents, teachers, and students that those skills should be mastered by all students at that grade level. If the student does not master these items by the end of the year, it is assumed something must be wrong with the student. That message is not true. Some children do not yet have the foundation necessary for the successful growth of certain skills. By expecting developmentally delayed, immature, or culturally deprived students to progress without first mastering the necessary readiness skills, we set them up to fail, and deprive them of the joy of learning. Such a situation can negatively affect their entire educational future. We force many students onto a dead-end track.

What is the answer? Probably any report card consisting of a checklist is inappropriate and falls short of giving a true picture of a student's learning. No checklist can tell the whole story. A checklist can even be misleading. I would like to see reporting become an ongoing procedure that includes having parents frequently visit students' schools to see for themselves. Most of my students' parents take time from work to come to our classroom (employers seem more willing to allow time off in support of education).

Student portfolios, compiled by students and teachers together, along with teacher, student, and parent observations and anecdotal records, should perhaps be the main focus. Communication between teacher and parents about student progress should take the form of oral and written conversations, not checklists. Checklists are valuable when used by the teacher to focus the teaching and also are a helpful way to organize assessment, but they are not as appropriate for reporting progress.

Although I invested much time, thought, and effort into completing the new progress report, parents spent little time reading the report. Most parents had already spent a fair amount of time in our classroom. We had been talking on the telephone and in person. Their students had also been talking about their experiences at school throughout the quarter. But the most helpful aspect was having students write their own conference plan for parent-teacher conferences. These included information on what the students felt they had learned, areas in which they had improved, and areas in which they wanted to improve, including academics and behavior. The students shared those plans with their families during the conference. Acting as classroom tour guides, they took their families around the room to show and explain graphs, posted literature responses, classroom pets, and other things that were important to them. Parents proudly shared with me things their students were doing at home, such as reading and writing by choice, often late into the night! I shared short stories about successes at school. We barely looked at the progress reports. Once the families had taken the reports home and perhaps taken a closer look, no one even called with any comments or questions.

The progress report was used throughout the year until a new committee met in the summer to make changes. The members considered input from parents and teachers. Little was changed outside of the physical arrangement and method of marking.

I wonder if in time we will come to realize the most reliable and appropriate way to report student progress is a combination of portfolios and ongoing oral and written conversations among parents, teachers, and students. Change is difficult. We all used the traditional report card as students, and it may be hard, or even impossible, for some people to accept a different form of reporting. Time will tell.

Section Three

NEW REPORTING MODELS FOR SHARING INFORMATION

Chapter 8
Implementing a
New Vision

DEBBIE TOFFLEMIRE

My classroom over the last six years has acquired a new look. In the past I relied on the reading basal to plan my reading class. The students read the story, answered reading and vocabulary questions, and completed workbook assignments. Reading was an isolated class having no connection with social studies, math, science, or language. Today, I examine the sixth-grade curriculum and carefully note what concepts I should teach. The selection of children's literature guides me to teach those concepts the students must learn. The concepts taught with literature are not just reading and answering questions, but problem solving in math and social studies, interpreting and analyzing information in science and language, and reporting and classifying in social studies and science. A language arts program that uses children's literature to teach *many* concepts has become a vital springboard to encourage student learning in my classroom.

Each day my sixth-grade students meet in pairs or collaborate in groups to plan the next steps in showing how they use information and resources to present newly acquired knowledge. Student collaboration, student self-selection, and student self-reflection are becoming the core of instructional activities. My teaching philosophy is based on a print-rich environment that prompts students to explore many areas of study. Students are reading to research, writing to orally share finished pieces, and listening to hear other student authors' styles. Each content area is carefully integrated into the reading program, thereby allowing the student to see a purpose for reading and writing. A literature-based program gives meaning and pleasure to the reading process, finally making skill instruction meaning-ful—and empowering both teachers and students (Trelease 1985). I am comfortable with the idea that the basal is not the only way to teach read-ing and enjoy watching the students as they select the texts to find informa-tion and choose their own projects to show skill application (Holdaway et al. 1989).

The change in my teaching philosophy has been a gradual process over the last several years. My beliefs reflect the influence of inspiring pre-senters, thought-provoking professional literature, and inquiring students. As my philosophy became increasingly reflected in my classroom, I found myself losing the spot at the front of the class. I became a rover, listening to students' conversations to determine what kind of facts would support a particular purpose. As time went on, my watching and listening increased and I delighted in hearing the questions students were asking themselves and one another. At times it became necessary to intervene when students developed too many choices for themselves and became stumped. I asked them to prioritize events, materials, and activities, and select only what would support their project and be possible to implement. On other occa-sions, I acted as a resource person, providing reading materials and sup-plies to move the final products toward completion.

It was during these moments that I began jotting down events: how par-ticular students asked to consult certain resources, or how long it took a group to sift out pertinent facts. I noticed that certain students who were quiet in a large class suddenly were contributing information and ideas for discussion. I observed the process in each group and looked forward to the time when the final product would unfold.

As I compiled more and more anecdotal information, I realized that the traditional reporting system did not address the kinds of learning that were occurring. I had observed students' process from start to finish and learned more about them than I ever had before. But could I distill all of this infor-mation into a single letter grade?

Having engaged students in learning by allowing them to make their own observations, select their own resources, and plan their own projects, I wondered what type of reporting method I should use to communicate everything students had learned.

What began as a small pad of notes randomly written about various stu-dents now became useful information that could be clearly organized into specific outcomes and used to direct instruction. The notes specifically ad-dressed how a student made progress toward a particular outcome and also documented the student's weaknesses. This information would reveal to the parents and myself how much the student had actually accom-plished. It identified which outcomes required additional instruction, and it helped parents understand the assigning of a particular letter grade. However, the letter grade alone was not sufficient to indicate what a student was able to do. The grade also did not show how progress had been measured, nor did it reward student effort (Hawkins 1993). Questions remained: How do you report to parents in a meaningful way students' progress toward a specific learning task? Could specific outcomes be developed in a way that allowed an appropriate reporting method to be designed?

A group of teachers in the district came together to discuss similar reporting concerns. Was every third-grade teacher in the district teaching to the same outcomes even though every teacher did not read *Charlotte's Web* as a class novel? By what set of standards were thematic units being developed? To what degree were teachers expecting the students to progress toward the outcome?

During this time I was beginning my second year as a writing trainer, providing staff development for teachers on the Six Trait Analytical Writing Model (Spandel & Stiggins 1990). This model states specific traits students need to learn. My job was to train teachers how to identify the traits in students' writing and teach students to use these traits. The scoring criteria identified the standards for acceptable performance. Teachers can all agree on acceptable criteria for scoring writing and use the criteria to consistently rate a writing piece with the same score throughout a building, district, or state. Teachers can also design criteria to assess instructional activities. Scoring criteria must be definitive to ensure that everyone understands what is expected (Herman, Aschbacher & Winters 1992).

It was at this time that I began collaborating with several other teachers who were grappling with the same issues. A sixth-grade teacher, a fourth-grade teacher, and I condensed our language outcomes to three reading and three writing outcomes, and drafted a reporting system using these outcomes (see Figures 8–1 and 8–2).

We received approval for a one-year pilot program to use an outcomes based language arts progress report. Approval of the pilot program was given with the condition that we also continue using the district-adopted traditional report card for the other subjects. Although we still maintained a letter grade, the outcome reporting system helped parents and teachers understand what the letter grade represented.

The real work lay ahead: development of a friendly management system to quickly record student progress. I called it a "progress notebook." Using a three-ring binder and my class list, I charted the columns with the student's name and the three outcomes across the top. It was important to list each student's name so that when I saw blank spaces I knew I had not observed or recorded any information for that student. With this type of

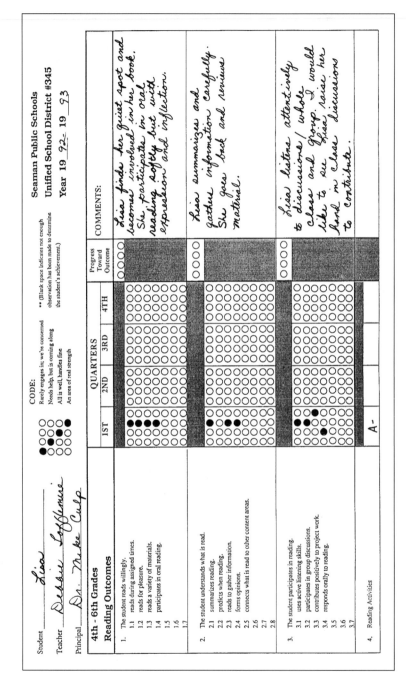

Figure 8-1 *Reading Outcomes*

Student Michael

Teacher *[signature]*

Principal

Seaman Public Schools
Unified School District #345
Year 19 _92_ - 19 _93_

CODE:
○○○○ Rarely engages in; we're concerned
○○○● Needs help, but is coming along
○○●● All is well, handles fine
●○○○ An area of real strength

** (Blank space indicates not enough observation has been made to determine the student's achievement.)

4th - 6th Grades
Writing Outcomes

Writing Outcomes	1ST	2ND	3RD	4TH	COMMENTS:
1. The student writes willingly.					Michael prewrites and begins several sentences then revises as he writes. When he doesn't have much to write about a topic he chooses another and tries to develop detail.
1.1 writes during assigned times.					
1.2 writes for a variety of reasons.					
1.3					
1.4					
1.5					
2. The student communicates through writing.					Michael is beginning to add more detail in his writing. He is working to limit his stories to one idea. He relies on simple, everyday words in his stories.
2.1 uses good word choice.					
2.2 develops an idea well.					
2.3 organizes writing.					
2.4 uses conventions appropriately.					
2.5					
2.6					
2.7					
3. The student publishes own writing.					Michael could improve his editing and bring his writing to closure with the help of a spell check on computer. He could final final drafts on the computer at school.
3.1 takes writing project to closure.					
3.2 uses a variety of forms.					
3.4 shares writing with an audience.					
3.5					
3.6					
3.7					
4. Writing Activity	C-				

Figure 8-2 *Writing Outcomes*

record system, I would need to consistently discipline myself to complete student observations. Each day, as the students were reading, writing, or working in groups, I would log my findings for the students I was observing. If I had not made an entry for a student that day, I knew I had to log the entry on the next available observation (see Figure 8–3).

When it was time to determine a reading or writing grade, I still relied on the grades accumulated in the grade book. However, in addition to the grade, I now had specific anecdotal information about how the students were making progress toward the outcome. The grade, although insignificant to me, was still recorded on the new report system. Now, during a parent conference, I felt I could give a complete evaluation of the student with or without a letter grade. This type of recording provided the most specific information to the parents and the students regarding progress, in spite of all the tedious hours of record management and preparing reports.

When we three teachers sat down in early summer, we noted several similarities about the new report system. First, we all agreed that although we still needed to develop a workable information management system, every piece of information we collected was valuable in assessing student performance. Secondly, we became aware of specific weaknesses in student performance. When work samples indicated unacceptable performance, it was possible to focus on appropriate remediation. Last of all, we learned that it was possible to communicate information about student learning to parents and administrators accurately. More importantly, if given the opportunity, progress could be reported without using a grade.

Teachers who also had changed their methods of instruction were ready to join us in experimenting with reporting systems that matched their methods. Teachers who were still very traditional were encouraged by the district at this time to make changes in their teaching practices so they could move toward a new reporting system. Teachers also looked at the district report card closely, finding that the curriculum only vaguely aligned with the reporting system. The report card also did not indicate all the areas teachers valued as significant within the framework of the changes they had made in their instructional methods. The curriculum did not specifically address an acceptable level of performance toward outcomes. Teachers who had made changes in their instructional practices were eager for an opportunity to draft a reporting system that measured student progress and effort.

In response to these concerns, a committee was established by the district to design a language arts curriculum aligned with district and state outcomes. The group developed five outcomes and diligently worked to draft a list of indicators that students would be required to perform at an acceptable level to meet the outcomes. A rubric was also designed to assist

STUDENT OBSERVATION FORM

NAME /DATE	READS WILLINGLY	UNDERSTANDS WHAT IS READ	PARTICIPATES IN READING
MATT D.	9-16-92 finishes work quickly to read		10-26-92 volunteered in class discussion
RANDY	10-6-92 reads after daily work is finished	10-28-92 recopies journal entry	10-28-92 difficulty answering questions correctly
BRAD	10-5-92 book is out when work is finished		10-28-92 actively engages in class discussion
SUSAN	10-15-92 becomes involved in her book	10-19-92 excellent summary with book review	
SARAH	9-16-92 reading but during instruction	10-30-92 reading folder questions are vague	10-26 / 10-28-92 seldom volunteers in class discussion
DANIEL	10-16-92 book review orally reads to class	10-19-92 Great deal of information in book review	
ANNA		10-30-92 deep thought, insight in reading questions	10-27-92 willingly shares opinion in discussion
MICHAEL	10-27-92 seldom has time except at silent reading	10-19-92 has to be called on afraid to answer	
JAMIE	10-20-92 expressions says she enjoys reading		
HOLLY		10-16-92 well-rounded summary in book review	

Figure 8–3 *Student Observation Form*

LANGUAGE ARTS EXIT OUTCOMES AND INDICATOR STATEMENTS
for K-6

1. Students actively engage in reading for pleasure and pursue reading for knowledge.

   Indicators
   - Uses reading skills effectively.
   - Gathers information from print, non-print and technological resources.
   - Understands what is read and makes connections.
   - Participates in reading activities.
   - Chooses materials appropriate for purpose and reading ability.
   - Reads a variety of materials.

2. Students actively construct writing for a variety of purposes.

   Indicators
   - Uses writing skills effectively.
   - Uses writing to communicate.
   - Participates in writing activities.
   - Chooses appropriate style for audience or purpose.
   - Writes in a variety of forms.

3. Students interact effectively in listening and speaking activities for a variety of purposes.

   Indicators
   - Participates in a variety of speaking activities as a member of a class or group.
   - Participates in variety of listening activities as a member of the class or a group.

4. Students demonstrate the ability to solve problems independently.

   Indicators
   - Plans strategies to address problems.
   - Investigates problems.
   - Critiques and refines strategies and/or products to resolve problems.
   - Communicates reasons to justify findings.

Figure 8–4 *Language Arts Exit Outcomes and Indicator Statements*

teachers in assessing the level of student performance toward each outcome (see Figure 8–4).

My colleagues and I decided to revise our language arts report system using the new outcomes. Our focus was to provide, in an effective manner, the most useful information to students, parents, other teachers, and administrators. The committee agreed it was important for teachers, parents, and students to understand the level of performance that grades represented.

Our duty in the months ahead would be to educate our district's parents and teachers, familiarizing them with the outcomes, indicators, and a

LANGUAGE ARTS RUBRICS FOR ASSESSING K-6 EXIT OUTCOMES

Outcome

1. Students actively engage in reading for pleasure and pursues reading for knowledge.

Indicator	High Quality	Acceptable Quality	Unacceptable Quality
Uses reading skills effectively	• Uses appropriate reading strategies (such as phonics, structural analysis, context clues, etc.) to gain understanding of text.	• Uses teacher directed reading strategies to gain understanding of text.	• Does not apply reading strategies and/or unable to gain meaning from text.
Gathers information from print, non-print and technologic resources	• Gathers accurate information from several resources. • Selects and uses written materials to expand their knowledge. • Reads technical information and applies knowledge.	• Gathers mostly accurate information from a limited variety of resources. • Uses assigned written materials to expand their knowledge. • Reads technical information but needs assistance to apply.	• Seldom gathers accurate information or fails to complete activity. • Seldom uses assigned written materials to expand their knowledge. • Unable to apply information from technical reading.
Understands what is read and makes connections.	• Draws accurate conclusions and explains. • Interprets clearly with justification and summarizes with rich detail and effective sequence. • Transfers knowledge from text or previous experiences to new or different situations.	• Draws accurate conclusions but has difficulty giving reasons. • Summarizes with sufficient detail and usually in sequential order. • Needs teachers guidance to transfer knowledge from text or previous experiences to new or different situations.	• Draws irrelevant, inaccurate, or no conclusion. • Summary lacks pertinent details, contains many inaccurate facts, or is not in sequential order. • Unable to transfer knowledge learned from text or previous experiences to new or different situations.
Participates in reading activities	• Willingly reads during assigned times. • Completes reading activities accurately and on time. • Actively participates in group discussions. • Willingly assumes different roles in group activities. • Consistently chooses to do extension activities.	• Reads during assigned times with teacher encouragement. • Completes assigned activities accurately and usually on time. • Participates in group discussion. • Performs assigned role in group activity. • Sometimes chooses to do extension activities.	• Reluctant to read and needs continuous prompting. • Rarely completes assignments. • Off task or distracting others during group discussions. • Chooses unassigned role or fails to participate in group activity. • Rarely or never chooses to do extension activities.
Chooses materials appropriate for purpose and reading ability	• Self selects materials appropriate for purposes and reading ability.	• Chooses appropriate materials with some guidance.	• Consistently chooses inappropriate materials for purpose.
Reads a variety of materials	• Chooses and reads a variety of materials.	• Reads from a variety of assigned materials.	• Reads from a limited variety of materials.

DRAFT 1993

Figure 8–4 *(Continued)*

LANGUAGE ARTS RUBRICS FOR ASSESSING K-6 EXIT OUTCOMES

2. Students actively construct writing for a variety of purposes.

Indicator	High Quality	Acceptable Quality	Unacceptable Quality
Uses writing skills effectively.	• Consistently transfers writing skills to new and different situations. • Varies beginnings and lengths of complete sentences in writing. • Consistently uses effective punctuation and capitalization. • Spelling is generally correct even on difficult words. • Grammar and Usage are generally correct given the purpose of the writing. • Words are accurate, strong, and specific. • Gives appropriate feedback and assistance about writing to peers. • Edits own work and makes most necessary changes. • Evaluation of own work shows deep reflection. • Organizes technical information and writes it in a clear form.	• Has some transference of writing skills to new and different situations. • Varies beginnings and lengths of complete sentences in writing with occasional guidance. • Uses correct punctuation and capitalization. • Spelling is generally correct. • Occasional problems in grammar and usage disrupt the flow of writing. • Words are very general or ordinary ("Words will do"). • Gives some appropriate feedback and assistance about writing to peers. • Edits own work and makes some necessary changes. • Evaluation of own work shows surface reflection, with guidance. • Needs assistance to organize and write technical information in a clear form.	• Seldom transfers writing to new and different situations. • Sentence beginnings and lengths are repetitive. • Sentences are incomplete. • Punctuation and capitalization are random and confused. • Spelling errors tend to be frequent even on common words. • Errors in grammar and usage are frequent and tend to be very noticeable. • Words are vague and flat. • Gives little or inappropriate feedback and assistance about writing to peers. • Seldom edits own work. • Unable to evaluate own work. • Technical writing is unclear.
Uses writing to communicate.	• Clearly and effectively communicates ideas in writing. • Ideas are organized effectively in written work. • Writing includes many elements of originality and liveliness.	• Communicates ideas in writing. • Ideas are organized in a logical sequence in written work. • Writing includes some elements of originality.	• Rarely or ineffectively communicates ideas in writing. • Ideas lack organization in written work. • Writing is flat, lifeless, and mechanical.
Participates in writing activities.	• Willingly writes during assigned times. • Completes writing accurately and on time. • Willingly shares and responds to writing. • Constantly publishes.	• Completes writing with some teacher encouragement. • Completes writing accurately usually on time. • Shares and responds to writing with some prompting. • Publishes with minimal teacher encouragement.	• Reluctant to write and needs continuous prompting. • Rarely completes writing. • Rarely shares or responds to writing or does so inappropriately. • Publishes only with teacher encouragement.
Chooses appropriate style for audience or purpose.	• Self-selects and used appropriate style for audience or purpose.	• Uses appropriate style for audience and purpose with some teacher assistance.	• Consistently chooses inappropriate style for audience or purpose.
Writes in a variety of forms.	• Chooses and writes in a variety of forms (such as: poetry, letters, fiction, nonfiction, etc.)	• Writes in a variety of forms when assigned.	• Writes in a limited variety of forms.

Figure 8–4 *(Continued)*

LANGUAGE ARTS RUBRICS FOR ASSESSING K-6 EXIT OUTCOMES

3. Students interact effectively in listening and speaking activities for a variety of purposes.

Indicator	High Quality	Acceptable Quality	Unacceptable Quality
Participates in a variety of speaking activities as a member of a class or group.	• Voluntarily speaks during appropriate times. • Shares well developed, pertinent information.	• Speaks at appropriate times with teacher encouragement. • Most information shared is pertinent.	• Reluctant to speak or speaks at inappropriate times. • Shares unrelated or distracting ideas.
Participates in variety of listening activities as a member of the class or a group.	• Uses effective non-verbal cues. (eye contact, facial expression, posture) • Listens attentively and interacts with speaker when appropriate. • Uses effective non-verbal feedback (eye contact, facial expression, posture).	• Uses appropriate non-verbal cues. • Most of the time listens attentively and may not interact with speaker. • Uses appropriate non-verbal feedback.	• Non-verbal cues missing or used inappropriately. • Off task while others are speaking. • Non-verbal feedback is missing or used inappropriately.

4. Students demonstrate the ability to solve problems independently.

Indicator	High Quality	Acceptable Quality	Unacceptable Quality
Plans strategies to address problems.	• Develops a plan containing the critical details needed to address problems.	• Has some ideas for developing a plan but is missing some details which make it workable.	• Requires much assistance to develop a plan.
Investigates problems.	• Investigates the workability and appropriateness of various strategies.	• Investigates obvious strategies.	• Rarely investigates the workability and appropriateness of strategies.
Critiques and refines strategies and/or products to resolve problems.	• Generates many possible strategies and/or solutions. • Works with persistence for workable solutions. • Self evaluates strategies used and applies knowledge and inferences.	• Finds one or two acceptable strategies and/or solutions. • Generally works with persistence for workable Draft 1993 solutions. • Evaluates strategies but only applies literal knowledge.	• Requires much assistance to go beyond the obvious. • Quits when solution not readily available. • Does not evaluate strategies for appropriateness and does not apply knowledge from previous experiences and explorations.
Communicates reasons to justify findings.	• Explains reasons clearly and logically to justify findings.	• Communicates the findings but has some difficulty in explaining them.	• Has difficulty communicating the findings and explaining reasons.

Figure 8–4 *(Continued)*

rubric. In addition, teacher support groups, site-council meetings, and district staff development would serve as resources to acquire more data about how this reporting system was working.

Soon our curriculum package was ready to be viewed in draft form (see Figure 8–5). Committee presentations to the school board and their approval were necessary before the committee could bring the new document to public attention. The board approved the language arts outcomes provided that the reporting system was attached as an addendum to the traditional report card. The staff in each building would decide whether it wished to use the new reporting system. The language arts committee would encourage other curriculum committees to design curriculum using a similar framework.

As many of our districts' schools already were working on drafting building outcomes, this document assisted those buildings in completing language arts outcomes. Soon all buildings agreed the document provided the necessary information needed to communicate language outcomes to students and parents.

The teachers in our district have tried to establish a set of criteria that connects closely to our methods of instruction and to design a reporting system that offers significant information. Teachers in other states have also pursued this goal. Rhode Island's Pilot Project, which began in 1989, developed a format for reporting indicators of a student's progress toward reaching the state's proposed literacy outcomes. Reports should be more descriptive than just a row of numbers. Although some reports will still include numbers, it is vital to determine what those numbers should represent (Maeroff 1991).

In Littleton, Colorado, when students at Mark Twain Elementary School began moving into an assessment program that would be based on the actual performances of students, the district devoted a great deal of time to developing criteria for scoring the performances. The district discovered it was easier to propose outcomes than it was to set the criteria and establish the performance levels represented by various achievements. The criteria must be understandable if students are to become responsible for their own learning (Maeroff 1991).

The assessment committee in our district may believe its work is nearly finished. In reality, the work has just begun to design a reporting system that most effectively measures progress and effort. As practitioners, we hope we have turned research and theory into curriculum and methodology, and, consequently, into learning experiences for students (Goodman 1992).

LANGUAGE ARTS PROGRESS REPORT

Year 19 _93_ - 19 _94_

Seaman Public Schools
Unified School District #345

Grades 3-6

Student _____Matthew_____

Teacher _____Debbie Fofflemire_____

Principal _____

CODE:

- Indicator not yet met
- Indicator met at acceptable level
- Indicator met at highly acceptable level
- ** (Blank space indicates not enough observation has been made to determine the student's achievement.)

Program Outcomes	Progress Toward Outcome			
	QUARTERS			
	1ST	2ND	3RD	4TH
1. Student actively engages in reading for pleasure and pursues reading for knowledge.				
• Uses reading skills effectively.				
• Gathers information from print, non-print and technological resources.				
• Understands what is read and makes connections.				
• Participates in reading activities.				
• Chooses materials appropriate for purpose and reading ability.				
• Reads a variety of materials.				
•				
2. Student actively constructs writing for a variety of purposes.				
• Uses writing skills effectively.				
• Uses writing to communicate.				
• Participates in writing activities.				
• Chooses appropriate style for audience or purpose.				
• Writes in a variety of forms.				
•				
3. Student interacts effectively in listening and speaking activities for a variety of purposes.				
• Participates in a variety of speaking activities as a member of a class or group.				
• Participates in variety of listening activities as a member of the class or a group.				
•				
4. Student demonstrates the ability to solve problems independently.				
• Plans strategies to address problems.				
• Investigates problems.				
• Critiques and refines strategies and/or products to resolve problems.				
• Communicates reasons to justify findings.				

COMMENTS: 1st Quarter - Writing ! Matthew is working to develop details in his stories. He uses simple words in his writing and has difficulty self-editing.

Figure 8–5 *Language Arts Progress Report*

COMMENTS | 1st Quarter - Reading / Matthew will continue to practice selecting important information from literature and non-fiction.

2nd Quarter - Reading / Matthew works to provide accurate information. At times he relies on direction to sort out information.
Writing / Matthew is providing more detail and is using some strong words in his writing. He has made attempts to self-edit. Voice and organization will require more time and practice with writing.

COMMENTS | 3rd Quarter - The extra time Matthew takes to reread and ask questions has helped him perfect his work. He continues to edit writing / reading.

4th Quarter - In reading and writing Matthew has become selective to what goes into a reading project or piece of writing. He provides facts from sources which support his work.

Draft 1993

Figure 8–5 (Continued)

REFERENCES

Farr, R. 1992. "Putting It All Together: Solving the Reading Assessment Puzzle." *The Reading Teacher* 46 (1):26–37.

Goodman, K. 1992. "I Didn't Found Whole Language." *The Reading Teacher* 46 (3): 188–198.

Gusky, T. 1993. "Issue." *Update* 35 (7):7.

Hawkins, V. 1993. "Issue." *Update* 35 (7):7.

Herman, J. L., P. R. Aschbacher, & L. Winters. 1992. "Setting Criteria." In *A Practical Guide to Alternative Assessment,* ed. R. S. Brandt. Alexandria, VA: Association for Supervision and Curriculum Development.

Tunnell, Michael & Jacobs, James. 1989. "Using *Real* Books: Research Findings on Literature Based Reading Instruction." *The Reading Teacher* 42 (7):470–477.

Maeroff, G. I. 1991. "Assessing Alternative Assessment." *Phi Delta Kappan* 73 (4): 273–281.

Trelease, J. 1985. "Using *Real* Books: Research Findings on Literature Based Reading Instruction." *The Reading Teacher* 39 (2):188–198.

Chapter 9
Telling the Story: Narrative Reports

KATHY EGAWA AND TARA AZWELL

Terry Johnson (1994) states, "Reporting involves conveying to parents, the child and to other professionals who have a need to know a balanced, coherent summary of the child's habitual range of performance, progress and promise as they pertain to the goals of the educational system." He identifies two essential elements of successful reporting systems:

- a sustained conversation among the child, the child's parent, and the teacher
- a sustained, balanced, critical written judgement that summarizes like performance, progress, and promise expressed in a prose passage

In Chapter 11, Lisa Biteau describes the process she uses to foster a sustained conversation among the child, parent, and teacher. This chapter demonstrates some strategies teachers have developed to create effective narrative reports.

CHARACTERISTICS OF SUCCESSFUL LEARNERS

Johnson (1994) reported that teachers, educational mission statements, research, and employers were in agreement about the characteristics of successful learners. The characteristics he identified were the following: knowledgeable, self-esteem, thoughtful, industrious, generative, empathetic, risk taker, and strategic. Narrative reports that address these characteristics provide a well-rounded picture of student learning.

NEGOTIATED NARRATIVE REPORTS

Anthony et al. (1991) described a process used by Canadian teachers to develop a reporting system that students, parents, and teachers found to be effective and helpful. The procedure they recommended included the following steps:

1. Involve teachers and administrators in discussions of proposed modifications to the reporting procedures.
2. Introduce negotiated narrative reports to parents at an informational meeting.
3. Approximately three weeks before the reports are to be written, send parents a letter fully detailing the procedure and requesting that they indicate areas of interest or concern.
4. Make a note of parents' requests and take them into account when writing report cards and preparing for conferences.

Anthony et al. (1994) provide a very helpful discussion of this process in Chapter 11 of their book *Evaluating Literacy: A Prospective for Change.* Sample materials for each step of the process are provided. Teachers involved in the research project were at first concerned about the kinds of information they believed parents would ask to receive. They were surprised by the actual responses of the parents:

- Parents placed more value on the anecdotal comment sections of the report cards than they did on marks, grades, and symbols.
- Very few parents wanted comparative information.
- Parents wanted early warning of problems and sufficient information to judge their children's progress toward desired outcomes.
- Parents wanted information about risk taking, self-monitoring, and reflection.

As Hogan describes in Chapter 3 of this book, narrative reports can be used successfully with students from diverse backgrounds, and she provides models of narrative reports.

NARRATIVE REPORTS AS DRAFTS: CONTINUING OUR INQUIRY INTO MEANINGFUL ASSESSMENT

Educators within the Indiana University community have explored the use of narrative reports for several years (Egawa 1994; Egawa & Edwards 1994; Egawa 1995). Carolyn Burke helped a group of teachers focus their efforts by combining indicators with narrative reports. By consciously considering the indicators of success or expectations for their classrooms, these teachers provided the students and parents with both a well-defined picture of classroom expectations and a personal, intimate look at each child as a learner. Kathy Egawa describes aspects of their process here.

Beginning in 1991, as part of a school restructuring effort, several Bloomington area teachers became responsible for eliminating letter grades and replacing them with narrative reports. The teachers began at the blank computer screen and literally began to write. The first reports averaged four legal-length pages per student. The comments, organized by subjects, alternated between the reporting period curriculum activities, teacher expectations, and the student's performance. Here is a brief example from one report:

> *Language Arts*
> I am very pleased with the increased interest and improvement that Leon has made in reading. A couple weeks ago he had two books ready to read with me after recess. I was so impressed. He has really gotten into the Mercer Mayer books lately, i.e., *Just a Mess*. We have been reading the book *Charlie and the Chocolate Factory* together. You might check it out from the library to finish with him. I have attached a paper that shows the "stages" a child progresses through when learning to read. Leon has shown incredible improvement. I feel that he demonstrated characteristics of both the first two stages when the year started and now is demonstrating characteristics from the next two. Leon can write and read back his own work, pick out some individual words and most letters now, read predictable books, is becoming more excited about reading and wants to read to others often; most important, he realizes that words have meaning . . .

Although everyone acknowledged that teachers knew their students better than ever before, the first narrative reports were unwieldy for both parents and teachers. Many parents in the community were not confident readers, and the new reporting form required a lot of reading. In addition, the information wasn't organized such that indications of the students' ability and success were clear. Despite the lengthy and informative reports, several parents continued to ask, "How is she doing?" Somewhat more common, however, was a lack of response to the report cards. This was unexpected, considering the time and energy it took to write the quarterly narratives. As teachers, we knew something needed to change.

During the second year of the restructuring efforts, the school leadership team responded to teachers' wishes to schedule goal-setting conferences in the fall and spring, with the narrative reports to come out in January and June. This provided us additional time during the fall to think more carefully about our own beliefs and expectations, as well as to consider feedback from parents. At Carolyn Burke's suggestion, we focused our initial efforts on listing indicators for the various curricular areas of the curriculum. Comments that the teacher had included under the lengthy "Language Arts" section were now divided into curriculum engagements: Classroom Newspaper, Newsboard, Dialogue Journal, Personal Journal, Literature Study, Buddy Reading, and Reading Strategies. Here is the first-draft wording of indicators for Dialogue Journal and Reading Strategies:

Dialogue Journal:

- uses written language and art to express ideas
- increases the amount s/he reads on his/her own over time (vs. each day asking "What does this say?")
- participates in a conversation by contributing more than brief responses to a partner's or teacher's questions
- spelling, punctuation, and handwriting become more conventional over time

Reading Strategies:

- uses picture cues to help read
- uses predictable word and story patterns to help read
- when comes to something s/he doesn't know uses meaning, letter/sound relationships, and language structure to help

Specific comments about each child were included below these statements. Three of us worked on the indicators, and the first draft was used with students in multi-age first- and second-grade classrooms. The responses from parents were heartening:

> Now I understand what's expected of the children!
>
> We feel this was a thorough progress report. We also need to set up a conference with you. The indicators were excellent and we do appreciate so much all that you are doing for Ellie this year. Thank you for your comments about her.
>
> The indicators were a great help. I've often wondered how you used each item to assess. It shows how much individual time is given! Erik doesn't have a comment so I am enclosing a couple of stories he has written at home. They are first copies but I thought you would like to see them. I would like them back. Thanks for all your hard work and time given. I'm very pleased.
>
> I am glad to see Donny is making some progress. I'm hoping he will even do much better. We are trying to help him more at home. I do believe the way you laid out the report helped us.

Initially, we included space for comment from the teacher, the parents, and the student at the end of the report, yet one student's father squeezed comments along the margins of each description area. The addition of these comments brought new life and importance to the reporting frame we had spent hours writing. We were pleased that the report almost "begged" his response and immediately revised the format to include space for comment throughout.

All of the teachers involved in this "assessment inquiry" have continued to revise our first efforts; it is our goal that the reporting frame remain responsive to the interests and values of parents, as well as to our own increased knowledge of the learning process. When Kathy completed her graduate study and returned to the Seattle area, she continued working to develop a reporting system for her primary-age students that would accomplish two goals: to paint an intimate picture of each child's interests, strengths, and needs as a learner, and to help parents answer the question "How is she doing?" Figure 9–1 is the next evolution of the initial narrative frame previously described.

Carolyn Burke and Kathy, in partnership with other teachers, have continued to refine the reporting system by adding continuums that help parents understand both the experiential and developmental nature of learning. Figure 9–2 (Campbell-Hill & Ruptic 1994) provides a jumping-off point for many teachers as they consider a continuum for initial readers. Adding continuums can help parents see learning from a broader perspective, as abilities that evolve over time and in carefully constructed environments. Such continuums enable students, parents, and teachers to understand that learning is not segmented into grade-leveled experiences; rather, students show strengths in relation to their experiences, and these vary across what might have been traditionally viewed as "stages." As Billie Manderick (Chapter 7) is fond of saying, "We remove the false ceiling from children's learning." In addition, Kathy's current school community is seeking new ways to involve the students and parents in the construction of these reports. We, like Peter Johnston (1992, 324–326), acknowledge that:

- Report cards can be viewed as drafts. The format we use this year does not have to be the same for the next ten years or even for the next year. Computers have made it possible to change formats at will.
- Reports of student progress do not have to be written entirely by the teacher. The more we can involve students in the reporting of their own development, the more reflective and involved they will become in their learning. Involving parents is also beneficial.
- Reporting does not have to include grades or ratings of any kind. Grades do not serve children well and are best replaced by descriptive details of the child's development.
- The report does not have to be on a single piece of paper or include only written comments. Written reports can accompany video tapes, audio tapes, and samples of student work that together paint a rich portrait of a learner.

Primary Progress Report

Name _____   Class _____

Parents _____   Teacher _____

Reporting Period _____   Phone _____

Days Present _____ Absent _____   Tardies _____

Note to parents: *Under each area of curriculum I have listed indicators which I look for when assessing and evaluating students. Students should be demonstrating or working toward these goals. These indicators are on the left hand side of the report. Specific comments about your child are on to right of the indicators. ** These items will be emphasized in the spring.*

Learning & Social Skills

The members of our school community focus on the following:
- doing their personal best
- being trustworthy
- being truthful
- actively listening to others
- not "putting down" others

- contributes to the learning of other class members
- settles down quickly in appropriate area
- works cooperatively with others
- actively participates in discussions and projects
- takes responsibility for learning
- cleans up before starting the next activity
- respects classroom materials and the property of others
- pays attention when others are speaking

Personal comments are added here for each child:

Reading and the Language Arts

Activities of the curriculum included in this category include: classroom newspaper, dialogue journals, personal notebook and sketchpad, author's folders, literature study, literacy strategies and the arts (drama, music, art)

Classroom Newspaper

- volunteers stories to the weekly news
- contributes conventions (punctuation, spelling, calendar information, temperature, etc.) at teacher request
- joins in the re-reading or shared reading of the dictated news of classmates
- contributes his or her own writing to the second page*
- actively participates and pays attention while others share
- stays in place/seat
- illustrates his/her own news

The newspaper is created daily on a plastic overlay that is projected on a large screen. The students contribute information as the teacher writes.
Personal comments are added here for each child:

Parent Comments:

Figure 9–1 *Primary Progress Report*

Dialogue Journal
• uses written language and art to express ideas
• increases the amount s/he reads on his/her own over time (vs. each day asking, "What does this say?")
• participates in a conversation by contributing more than brief responses to a partner or teacher's questions
• spelling, punctuation, and handwriting become more conventional over time
Parent Comments:

Each student and the teacher correspond daily in a dialogue journal. The students and teacher read each other's messages and write responses. The classroom assistant provides help if needed. *Personal comments are added here for each child:*

Personal Notebook & Sketch Pad
• finds personally meaningful ideas to preserve in notebooks
• turns to next clean page and dates; works page by page
• uses art and writing (adds written text with the teacher's support if most entries are drawn
• takes new risks with his/her entries
• ideas --> pictures --> letters/words --> more elaborated ideas
• begins stories that can be added to author's folder*
• uses notebook to complete work begun in literature study groups, author's circles, inquiry projects
Parent Comments:

Each child has a personal notebook and sketch pad. These are used daily, both for the child's work and at the teacher's direction or suggestion. *Personal comments are added here for each child:*

Literature Study
• signs up for book of choice
• participates in discussion by 1) making personal connections with the story, 2) commenting and asking questions about the text and illustrations, 3) discussing with group members,
• listens to the story on tape and follows along
• contributes to the plans and extension activities**
• negotiates with friends how to share the book**
• follows along with the reading of the book (based on his/her own ability)
• reads book for homework**
• presents his/her ideas about the story to the class
Parent Comments:

Literature Study is an on-going engagement in the classroom. A new set of 4-5 books is presented every week or two; students sign up for a book of their choice and then meet daily with the teacher in discussion groups. *Personal comments are added here for each child:*

Figure 9–1 *(Continued)*

Literacy Strategies & Appropriate Strategy Instruction

When reading ...
• uses predictable word & story patterns
• uses illustrations
• uses letter/sound knowledge
• reads for meaning / expects what s/he reads to make sense

When writing ...
• risks writing what s/he is thinking rather than being over concerned with correct spelling
• uses multiple sources to help write his/her thoughts: friends, print around the room and in books, personal knowledge, adults.

Parent Comments:

Literacy strategies are highlighted daily in the classroom, specifically during the newspaper composition, shared reading activities, "Readers Club," and during journal writing. The teacher and teaching assistant both note and extend the strategies the students employ.
Personal comments are added here for each child:

Author's Folder**

• keeps track of interesting ideas to write about
• selects pieces from notebook/journal to add to folder for more extensive writing
• writes for an extended period of time (increases from 5-10 minutes to 30-40 minutes)
• keeps writing file organized*
• share writing with others (informally or by signing up for author's chair)*
• rereads to edit for meaning
• uses response comments from teacher and peers*
• uses available resources (word rings, posters, books) to help with spelling
• rereads to edit for conventions (as appropriate)*

Parent Comments:

Personal comments are added here for each child:

Mathematics

We have worked with the following concepts:	Your child as a mathematician:
• making connections between thinking in math and his/her own life	*Personal comments are added here for each child, as well as check marks next to concepts addressed during that reporting period.*
• manipulating objects (by teacher direction or own his/her own) to represent math processes	
• creating new ways to use math materials; makes connections beyond teacher direction	
• representing processes symbolically (w/ numerical equations, i.e. 8+6=14); reads math symbols and understands what is written	
• performs simple number operations (addition & subtraction) through 10	
• performs more complex operations:	
column addition	
2,3,4+ digit addition, subtraction	
addition and subtraction thru 18	
regrouping	
multiplication	
• money	
• time	
• measurement	**Math Club:** Your child has chosen to explore these math skills during small group strategy lessons:
• weight	
• reading graphs/graphing	
• shapes	
• understands mathematics as a tool that helps people get things accomplished	

Figure 9–1 *(Continued)*

Social Studies & Science Inquiry
** Note: based on both class-chosen topics and personally chosen topics

• identifies topics of interest*
• relates what s/he already knows about the topic and why the topic is personally interesting*
• identifies what s/he would like to know*
• finds and uses resources for study: people, books, movies, etc.*
• uses writing and drawing to preserve ideas and notes*
• organizes new information to share with others
• checks work for conventions (spelling, punctuation, capitalization)
• contributes to the strategies s/he needs (generating ideas, organizing information, editing. etc.)*
• shares through class presentations
• shares in writing*
• keeps an organized inquiry notebook

Parent Comments:

This year began with sharing favorite family , stories and explorations of our town, Redmond, WA. Students each created a project or artifact which highlighted what Redmond meant to them. Students are now involved in "expert projects," inquiring into a topic or subject of personal interest. *Personal comments are added here for each child:*

Library, Music & Physical Education
Comments from the school "specialists"

Library

Music

P.E.

Additional Teacher Comments

Parent Comments

Student Comments

Figure 9–1 *(Continued)*

Reading Continuum

Effort

Developing	Beginning	Expanding	Bridging	Fluent
• Sees self as reader. • Reads books with word patterns. • Knows most letter sounds. • Retells main idea of text. • Recognizes simple words. • Relies on print and illustrations.	• Reads early-reader books. • Relies on print more than illustrations. • Uses sentence structure clues. • Uses meaning clues. • Uses phonetic clues. • Retells beginning, middle, end. • Recognizes names/words by sight. • Begins to read silently. • Understands basic punctuation.	• Reads beginning chapter books. • Reads and finishes a variety of materials with frequent guidance. • Uses reading strategies appropriately. • Retells plot, characters, and events. • Recognizes different types of books. • Makes connections between reading, writing, and experiences. • Silent reads for short periods.	• Reads medium level chapter books. • Reads and finishes a variety of materials with guidance. • Reads and understands most new words. • Uses reference materials to locate information with guidance. • Increases knowledge of literary elements and genres. • Silent reads for extended periods.	• Reads most young adult literature. • Selects, reads and finishes a wide variety of materials. • Uses reference materials independently. • Understands literary elements and genres. • Begins to interpret deeper meaning in young adult literature with frequent guidance. • Participates in guided literary discussions.

Writing Continuum

Effort

Developing	Beginning	Expanding	Bridging	Fluent
• Takes risks with writing. • Begins to read own writing. • Writes names and favorite words. • Writing is from top-bottom, left-right, front-back. • May interchange upper and lower case letters. • Begins to use spacing between words. • Uses beginning, middle and ending sounds to make words. • Begins to write noun-verb phrases.	• Writes pieces that self and others can read. • Begins to write recognizable short sentences. • Writes about observations and experiences with some descriptive words. • Experiments with capitals and punctuation. • Forms many letters legibly. • Uses phonetic spelling to write independently. • Spells some words correctly. • Begins to revise by adding on.	• Begins to consider audience. • Writes pieces with beginning, middle and end. • Revises by adding description and detail. • Listens to peers' writing and offers feedback. • Edits for punctuation and spelling. • Uses capital letters and periods. • Forms letters with ease. • Spells many common words correctly.	• Begins to write for various purposes. • Begins to organize ideas in logical sequence. • Begins to develop paragraphs. • Begins to revise by adding literary devices. • Develops editing and proof reading skills. • Employs strategies to spell difficult words correctly.	• Uses appropriate tone and mood for a variety of purposes. • Experiments with complex sentence structure. • Connects paragraphs in logical sequence. • Uses an increased repertoire of literary devices. • Revises for clarity by adding reasons and examples. • Includes deleting in revision strategies. • Edits with greater precision (spelling, grammar, punctuation, capitalization).

Figure 9–2 *Developmental Continuum*

Johnston reminds us that in the end, "it is *the act of writing* a report that is important in coming to grips with, or pulling together, what you know about a child and in applying that to your instruction" (1992, 326). There is no substitute for teachers' understanding of the learning process; narrative comments reflect the opportunities that students meet in the classroom environments we create. As such, they are as much indicators of our values as they are of students' abilities (Harste 1993).

SUMMARY

Narrative reports are becoming a more common form of reporting to parents throughout the world. They provide the opportunity to identify and celebrate the unique characteristics of each learner, as well as to highlight what educators hold most valuable. They can be modified to provide the kind of information that is most helpful to each student, parent, and teacher. The report for each child can be easily personalized, especially with the assistance of computers.

However, writing effective narrative reports is a formidable task for teachers new to the process, as well as time-consuming for even the most experienced teachers. Kathy has found an inquiry process most valuable for all partners in the venture (Egawa 1994). Over time, groups of teachers can begin to identify the beliefs that drive both their teaching and reporting, and revise those during an ongoing journey of professional development. Technology offers one tool for making the writing task more manageable. Several authors included in this volume regularly use computer programs and electronic portfolios as tools for streamlining the process. Narrative reports are potentially rich opportunities to communicate information about learning and should be considered an integral part of any reporting system.

REFERENCES

Anthony, R., T. D. Johnson, N. Mickelson & A. Preece. 1991. *Evaluating Literacy: A Perspective for Change.* Portsmouth, NH: Heinemann.

Campbell-Hill, B. & C. Ruptic. 1994. *Practical Aspects of Authentic Assessment: Putting the Pieces Together.* New York, NY: Christopher-Gordon Press.

Egawa, K. 1994. *When Teachers Inquire.* Dissertation in progress, Indiana University, Bloomington, IN.

Egawa, K. & D. Edwards. 1994. Evaluating Literacy: The Beginnings of Parent-Teacher Collaboratives. Article. UKRA. Oxford, UK: Blackwell Publishers.

Egawa, K. 1995. "When Teachers and Parents Inquire." In *Creating Classrooms for Authors*, 2nd edition, ed. J. Harste and K. Short. Portsmouth, NH: Heinemann. In press.

Harste, J. 1993. "Literacy As Curricular Conversations About Knowledge, Inquiry, and Morality." In *Theoretical Models and Processes of Reading*, 4th edition, ed. M. Ruddell and R. Ruddell. Newark, DE: International Reading Association.

Johnson, T. 1994. "Evaluation and Assessment in the Classroom: The Tigers Kiss." Address to the Fourth Annual Kansas-Teachers Applying Whole Language Conference. January 22, 1994. Manhattan, KS.

Johnston, P. H. 1992. *Constructive Evaluation of Literate Activity.* Portsmouth, NH: Heinemann.

Chapter 10
An Alternative to Letter Grades

KIM YOUNG

T he change process begins at many different levels, including an individual teacher, a school, or an entire district. All routes of change are as effective as those people supporting change. There is no one right way to bring about improvements in education.

This chapter describes the travels of one elementary school down the road to a progress report without letter grades. Rather, it reports student progress toward outcomes. Rochester Elementary School developed the reporting system over a four-year period. This progress report evolved from comments and suggestions for improvement by teachers, parents, and administrators. The progress report continues to change every year according to the needs of the students and teachers, and the changing curriculum standards. The basic outline of the reporting system is a list of outcomes for each grade level. These are evaluated, and the results are communicated through descriptive phrases. The phrases are consistent from first through sixth grades. The outcomes are different, depending on the grade level.

The reporting system was developed from shared beliefs within the school community:

- Educators teach the child, not the curriculum.
- Students have some choices in their mode of learning.
- Students learn at different rates.
- Children don't fail.
- All children can learn.
- Students manipulate their environment.

- Educators promote higher-level thinking skills for transferable learning more than for the learning of isolated skills.

Because they were so widely held, it was agreed that our reporting system should reflect these beliefs. In this way, the Rochester Elementary School community began its journey toward a nongraded progress report.

YEAR ONE

- Teachers wrote exit outcomes for each grade level.
- Cross grade-level teachers convened to correlate outcomes.

In an attempt to match assessment with curriculum and teaching methods, the teachers began to look at the district curriculum and wrote down the exit outcomes for each grade level. The question was asked, "What do we expect from students in our classroom before they leave our grade level?" The responses were developed into outcomes, which were written in learning-objective format. The staff worked during faculty meetings and in-service days. The principal worked with the students three or four times throughout the year to give the teachers extra time to develop outcomes.

Next, teachers spent time with cross grade-level teachers. For example, the third-grade teachers met with the second- and fourth-grade teachers to check for coverage of the entire curriculum. They searched for holes or overlaps in outcomes. Then the teaching staff met as a group and correlated all six grade levels' outcomes. The focus was on format, headings, and wording. The outcomes were to follow the same format throughout the grades, but each grade would have different outcomes. During this year, teachers had no idea how the final product would look, or how it would be used. They were simply trying to outline their grade-level outcomes to use as a classroom guide through the curriculum.

YEAR TWO

- Teachers developed coding system for progress report (see Figure 10–1).
- Principal developed format for recording progress.
- School board approved pilot program.
- Parents and teachers began nine-week pilot of progress report.
- Parents and staff held meetings during pilot.
- Nine-week pilot report was presented to school board for approval for next school year.

3rd Grade Science/Social Studies

1.   **The learner will demonstrate growth in Social Studies**
      1.1   **Learn facts and concepts**
      1.2   **Learn map skills**
      1.3   **Participate in activities/discussions**

2.   **The learner will demonstrate growth in Science**
      2.1   **Learn facts and concepts**
      2.2   **Participate in activities/discussions**

3.   **The learner will demonstrate appropriate effort in art**

4.   **The learner will demonstrate appropriate behavior**
      4.1   **Accept responsibility for actions**
      4.2   **Is courteous and respectful to peer/adults**

5.   **The learner will demonstrate good work habits**
      5.1   **Listen carefully**
      5.2   **Follow directions**
      5.3   **Write legibly in daily work**
      5.4   **Uses time wisely/completes assignments on time**
      5.5   **Work quietly**
      5.6   **Work independently**
      5.7   **Work cooperatively as a group member**

Figure 10–1 *Third Grade Science/Social Studies*

The staff decided the outcomes were important for the students and would be used as a part of an assessment and reporting system shared with parents. A coding system was developed to use with the outcomes to relay to parents their child's movement toward the desired outcome. The principal developed a format and method for teachers to record the student's progress for each nine-week period. The coding system would visually show growth for each student in different areas (see Figure 10–2).

SECOND/THIRD GRADE LANGUAGE ART OBJECTIVES

Objective	Not ready to measure	Not showing necessary effort	No Progress	Slow Progress	Satisfactory Progress	Highly Satisfactory Progress
The learner will be introduced to a variety of quality literature and authors.						
1.1 TLW be able to identify the author and illustrator and title of a book.						
1.2 TLW distinguish between real and make-believe selections.						
1.3 TLW identify the characteristics of a fairytale.						
The learner will extend vocabulary.						
2.1 TLW show growth in differentiating between consonants and vowels.						
2.2 TLW show growth in recognizing vowel sounds.						
2.3 TLW recognize that all words have a standard spelling.						
2.4 TLW show growth in recognizing meanings of words.						
The learner will share ideas in an organized, written form.						
3.1 TLW write a simple sentence, using correct capitalization, periods and question marks.						
3.2 TLW show growth in correct usage of exclamation marks, commas, and apostrophes.						
The learner will be introduced to grammar skills and THEIR correct usage.						
4.1 TLW identify nouns and verbs.						
4.2 TLW identify singular and plural nouns.						
4.3 TLW identify adjectives.						
The learner will be introduced to the use of reference skills.						
5.1 TLW alphabetize words to the second letter.						
5.2 TLW demonstrate the use of guide words in locating a specific entry word in the dictionary.						
The learner will recognize elements of a story.						
6.1 TLW show growth in identifying main ideas, details, characters and setting in a short story.						
6.2 TLW show growth in sequencing events.						

1st quarter in blue
2nd quarter in yellow
3rd quarter in red
4th quarter in graphite

Achieving above the norm

Achieving near the norm

Achieving below the norm

Figure 10–2 *Second/Third Grade Language Art Objectives*

113

The next step was to gain the school board's approval of the progress report. Support of school board members would be crucial to changing a reporting system. School board members were certain to hear from parents with praise and complaints. To be able to defend their decision, they had to understand the purpose and reasons for the change. School board members learned about the project from research articles, brief presentations, and attendance at teacher in-service sessions.

The school board requested that a pilot program be set up for the last quarter of the year. Its members wanted to sample parents' response to the reporting system before committing to a larger project.

The pilot program consisted of two students of varying achievement levels from each classroom. The students were chosen by their teacher. At the beginning of the fourth quarter, letters were sent informing the parents of the pilot report system. A meeting was held for all parents and teachers participating in the pilot program. The principal discussed the report card and explained the reasons for changing to the new system.

Each child in the pilot program was given a new report card at three weeks and six weeks into the quarter. These reports enabled parents to compare the two new report cards in reflecting the progress of their child.

Another meeting was held with the parents after the second progress report to discuss the implications of and their feelings about the new reporting system. Parents were given a survey to complete at home and return in the next week (see Figure 10–3). That way, parents who were not comfortable speaking in front of large groups could verbalize their feelings about the progress report.

Following this meeting, using the information gained from the parent meeting and the surveys, the principal wrote a report to the school board. For the most part, parents' comments were very positive. Parents felt they had received a clearer picture of their child's progress. They were able to clearly see the outcomes (expectations) required before a child could exit each grade level. If the child was having difficulties in a certain area, the problems were easily identified with the new reporting system.

In May, the school board authorized a one-year pilot of the new progress report for all Rochester Elementary School students. The current district report would not be used at Rochester.

YEAR THREE

- Teachers updated the progress report.
- Teachers developed a system to keep record of students' progress.

**Parent Field Test Survey
for Rochester Report Card**

Please respond using a Likert Scale ranging from 1-5 with 1 = Strongly Disagree and 5 = Strongly Agree and 3 being neutral. Circle the numeral that best conveys your feeling.

The new report card gives me more information about the expectations for my child at his/her grade level.
(1..2..3..4..5..)

The new report card gives me more information about my child's progress in relation to grade level objectives.
(1..2..3..4..5..)

The new report card gives me more information that should help in a clearer dialogue between parent and teacher.
(1..2..3..4..5..)

The new report card gives me more information so I can constructively guide my child in setting his/her immediate educational goals.
(1..2..3..4..5..)

The new report card gives me more information so I can assist my child in planning for improvement in relative weak areas.
(1..2..3..4..5..)

Upon completion of six grades at Rochester or transfer from Rochester the new report card gives more information to the receiving school.
(1..2..3..4..5..)

The new report card is more student friendly.
(1..2..3..4..5..)

Figure 10–3 *Parent Field Test Survey*

- Copies of each grade level's objectives were sent home with students in the weekly school newsletter the first month of school.
- Parents continued to be informed and educated concerning nongrading.
- Teachers' interpretations of the coding system were discussed.
- Parent-teacher conferences were held, and the principal listened to parents' concerns.
- Parents gave feedback about the progress report.
- School board granted another one-year pilot of progress report.

Following the nine-week pilot, the staff gathered ideas and suggestions from parents. These were incorporated into the progress report, which was used at the beginning of the year (Figure 10–4).

Many teachers struggled in the first quarter with the new assessment records, management techniques, and daily record keeping. They were familiar with the report, but using it required new record-keeping skills. Teachers wanted valuable information without using percentages. Several sharing and brainstorming sessions were conducted to determine possible solutions. Because each teacher had a personal record-keeping style, it took time to develop a system that was comfortable and reliable for everyone.

In the first month of school, the principal sent home a copy of each grade level's objectives from the progress report and a small sample of the new progress report. In a weekly newsletter, she discussed the reasons for the change in reporting systems and the format throughout the school year. Periodically, she reprinted research articles on nongrading versus grading and their effects on children.

After the first quarter, the staff conducted parent-teacher conferences. Many teachers found themselves discussing only the progress report during these conferences because parents had not been prepared well regarding the expectations on the report. Although efforts had been made to inform parents, many did not seem to understand the impact of the report until they actually received it at home.

The principal sat at a centrally located table to be easily available to hear parents' concerns regarding the progress report. That enabled the classroom teachers to concentrate on discussing the child's progress and not the report format. Then, at the next faculty meeting, the staff discussed parents' concerns and made needed adjustments. Parents could see that their comments and suggestions had a direct impact.

For the conference, teachers saved selected student work in a portfolio to demonstrate students' progress to parents. Teachers developed their own portfolio systems. Some selected the work themselves. Others selected some of the work and the student selected some. The teachers referred to these folders when completing progress reports and later for conferences with parents.

The teachers kept the work they were evaluating for the progress report in the student's portfolio. They also kept work from quarter to quarter to show a student's progress. It was difficult to show progress for some children each nine-week period because new outcomes were addressed each quarter. Students who had difficulties with new outcomes sometimes had performed better on old outcomes than they had the previous quarter. With a portfolio, we were able to show the child's progress over time versus a single assignment. And parents could more easily see children's progress through a portfolio than a reporting system.

Evidence of a child's progress toward outcomes was documented for parents through specific examples. For instance, if a child was having

Code :
       * first quarter   ∧ third quarter
       # second quarter   O fourth quarter

NAME: Michael   TEACHER: Mrs. Morris

First Grade Language Arts	Not ready to measure	Not showing necessary effort	No progress	Slow progress	Satisfactory progress	Highly satisfactory progress	Below, on, or above expected level	Comments
1. The learner will be introduced to a variety of quality literature and authors	//////	//////					//////	Michael reads a good variety of books. He will independently select fiction and nonfiction although he seems to prefer informational books about animals.
1.1 Be able to identify the author, illustrator, and title of a book or story		//////					//////	
2. The learner will extend his/her vocabulary					#	∧ O	//////	
2.1 Recognize letters have certain sounds					*∧	#	//////	
2.2 Identify and recognize the consonant sounds					*O	#	//////	Michael knows all of the letter sounds and begins to put those together to read words.
2.3 Recognize letters can be put together to make words					*		//////	
2.4 Understand all words have a standard spelling					#∧	O	//////	
2.5 Show growth in differentiating between consonants and vowels						O	//////	
2.6 Show growth in recognizing vowel sounds					#∧	O	//////	
2.7 Show growth in recognizing meanings of words					#∧	O	//////	
3. The learner will share ideas in an organized form	//////	//////			#∧		//////	
3.1 Share ideas verbally in an organized form					*#∧	O	//////	
3.2 Show growth in writing ideas in an organized and readable form					*#	∧ O	//////	
3.3 Show growth in the correct usage of capitalization, periods and question marks						O	//////	
4. The learner will be introduced to the correct use of grammar skills	//////	//////			#	∧ O	//////	
4.1 Show growth in using correct sentence structure	//////	//////			∧	O	//////	
5. The learner will be introduced to the use of reference skills	//////	//////					//////	Michael is beginning to recognize the setting of a story. Recalling details is a little more difficult for him.
5.1 Alphabetize words to the first letter					#∧	O	//////	
6. The learner will recognize elements of a story	//////						//////	
6.1 Show growth in identifying characters, details, setting and the main idea of a story					∧ O		//////	

Figure 10–4   *Progress Report*

NAME __Michael__   TEACHER __Mrs. Morris__

1st Math*	Not ready to measure	Not showing necessary effort	No progress	Slow progress	Satisfactory progress	Highly satisfactory progress	Below, on, or on expected level	Comments
1. The learner will grow in computation skills	\\\\\\\\	\\\\\\\\	\\\\\\\\	\\\\\\\\	\\\\\\\\		\\\\\\\\	
1.1 Count objects to 100				# 89-100	# achieved		\\\\\\\\	Michael can count objects up to 88 with little or no trouble. We will be practicing counting from 89-100
1.2 Read and write numbers from one through fifty					✗ achieved		\\\\\\\\	
1.3 Recall addition sums to 5					# ∧ O		\\\\\\\\	
1.4 Recall subtraction for differences to 5					∧ O		\\\\\\\\	
1.5 Accurately use addition and subtraction skills to 12					✗# ∧∧ # ∧∧		\\\\\\\\	
1.6 Show growth in understanding place value					O		\\\\\\\\	
1.7 Show growth in skip counting by fives and tens	#				∧ O		\\\\\\\\	
2. The learner will show growth in measurement skills	\\\\\\\\	\\\\\\\\	\\\\\\\\	\\\\\\\\	\\\\\\\\			
2.1 Use a ruler to measure an item in inches					∧ O		\\\\\\\\	
2.2 Show growth in telling time to the (hour) and (half-hour)					∧ σ		\\\\\\\\	
2.3 Show growth in writing time to the (hour) and half hour					∧ O		\\\\\\\\	
3. The learner will show growth in money skills	\\\\\\\\	\\\\\\\\	\\\\\\\\	\\\\\\\\	\\\\\\\\		\\\\\\\\	
3.1 Recognizing pennies, nickels, dimes, quarters, and dollar bills					O		\\\\\\\\	
3.2 counting coins to $0.25.					O		\\\\\\\\	
4. The learner will apply their knowledge of math to problem solving situations	\\\\\\\\	\\\\\\\\	\\\\\\\\	\\\\\\\\	\\\\\\\\		\\\\\\\\	
4.1 Show growth in solving one-step story problems involving additions and subtraction through 12					∧ O		\\\\\\\\	

Figure 10–4 *(Continued)*

NAME Michael TEACHER Mrs. Morris

1st Report	Not ready to measure	Not showing appropriate effort	No progress	Slow progress	Satisfactory progress	Highly satisfactory progress	Below, on, or above expected level	....	Comments	....
1. The learner will demonstrate progress							\\\\\\\\\\\\\\			
in handwriting										
1.1 Form letters correctly					*# Λ	O	\\\\\\\\\\\\\\			
1.2 Form numberals correctly					*# Λ	O	\\\\\\\\\\\\\\			
1.3 Write legibly in daily work					*# Λ	O	\\\\\\\\\\\\\\			
2. The learner will demonstrate progress							\\\\\\\\\\\\\\			
in social studies/science										
2.1 Learn concepts and facts					*# Λ	O	\\\\\\\\\\\\\\			
2.2 Participate in group activities					*# Λ	O	\\\\\\\\\\\\\\			
3. The learner will participate in art activities					*# Λ	O				
4. The learner will demonstrate appropriate							\\\\\\\\\\\\\\			
behavior and work habits										
4.1 Accept responsibility for actions					*#	Λ O	\\\\\\\\\\\\\\		Michael sh	ows
4.2 Practice self-discipline					*#	Λ O	\\\\\\\\\\\\\\		leadership	in the
4.3 Work cooperatively with others					*#	Λ O	\\\\\\\\\\\\\\		classroom	by
4.4 Listen carefully					*#	Λ O	\\\\\\\\\\\\\\		completing	his
4.5 Follow directions					*#	Λ O	\\\\\\\\\\\\\\		work on	time.
4.6 Use time effectively					*#	Λ O	\\\\\\\\\\\\\\			
4.7 Work independently					*#	Λ O	\\\\\\\\\\\\\\			
4.8 Take responsibility for materials					*#	Λ O	\\\\\\\\\\\\\\			
Attendance	1	2	3	4	Total					
Days present	47	42	43	41	173					
Days absent	0	3	1	3	7					
Times tardy	0	6	0	0	0					
Absences/tardies hindered progress										
(Mark with an * if applicable)										

Figure 10–4 *(Continued)*

difficulty with punctuation, then a writing sample was available to show this difficulty.

The students also chose one paper from their work each week and wrote a reflective paragraph about what they had learned from the assignment and their perception of their performance. Students chose papers they felt reflected their best work or an assignment they really enjoyed. Sometimes the teacher's choice and the student's choice were the same and other times they were different. The items in the portfolio could be organized according to the order of outcomes on the progress report to ensure a smooth transition during the conference.

Many teachers commented about how easy it was to prepare for conferences since assessment information was already organized. However, completing the progress report was time-consuming. Many teachers found that more handwritten comments were needed to explain their reasoning. Parents were very positive about the handwritten comments, and some even found the comments more helpful than the coding on the progress report.

At the same time, the teachers wrestled with the coding. Each person interpreted the codes differently, yet the goal was to alleviate a teacher's interpretive bias. During many faculty meeting discussions, teachers slowly worked through their misinterpretations. By the end of the school year, they had begun to feel comfortable with the report format.

As the third year ended, the school board was approached for an extension of the pilot. Many parents wanted to see the project continue, and a few wanted to see it end. Both groups were represented at the meeting. The teachers reported on the past year, presented proposed changes for next year's report, and asked for an extension. The board authorized the pilot for another year.

YEAR FOUR

- Teachers revised objectives and coding.
- Teachers had parent night in the first week of school.
- Parent-teacher conferences were held using the same format as the previous year.
- Printed articles concerning grades, competition, and alternative assessment were shared in weekly school newsletter.
- Teachers used weekly progress notes.
- The school began the outcomes education process for state assessment.
- An "at-risk" program was designed to tutor students who were not meeting progress report objectives.

- Parent and staff participated in a progress report forum.
- The school board approved a progress report.
- A summer school program was designed to tutor students who did not meet objectives from the progress report.

The faculty began the year by discussing positives and negatives from the previous year. It was decided to revise the coding system and make the objectives more understandable (see Figure 10–5).

Each teacher held a parent night the first week of school to explain the progress report's format and objectives and to discuss expectations for children at each grade level. Teachers also discussed discipline, classroom procedures, and special units to be studied during the year.

Although teachers were more confident about assessment and record keeping, and could more easily see the benefits to the new system, they continued to express concerns. These included student motivation, quality of student work, and consistency about expectations among teachers at the same grade level. To motivate students and improve the quality of their work, some teachers began sending weekly individual reports to parents informing them about the student's performance. Reward systems were built in for work turned in on time and quality work. These additions were a success with parents and students. Parents were aware of their child's progress before the nine-week report, and students knew exactly where they stood each week. Changes were also made in the coding on the progress report to clarify the intended message.

Use of the term *standards* in the coding was a problem. Some parents and teachers felt they understood this term, but others were uncomfortable with it. Parents also were concerned with the standards that had been selected and the process used to make those decisions. They did not want mediocrity. They did not want the teaching to stop once a student had met the standards. And they did not want students to work only toward minimum standards. For their part, teachers had difficulties deciding whether the standards were intended to be the same for every child regardless of ability. Teachers and parents struggled with these issues all year.

Teachers continued to listen to parents' comments and concerns about the progress report throughout the year. In the spring, parents were asked to complete a survey developed by the staff. Survey questions concerned student achievement, clarity of goals and objectives, assessment and accountability, teacher effectiveness, parental/community involvement, school leadership, and school climate.

Also in the spring, parents were invited to a progress report forum, at which they could publicly air their concerns and praise for the progress report. Parents, teachers, administrators, and board members all attended and spoke.

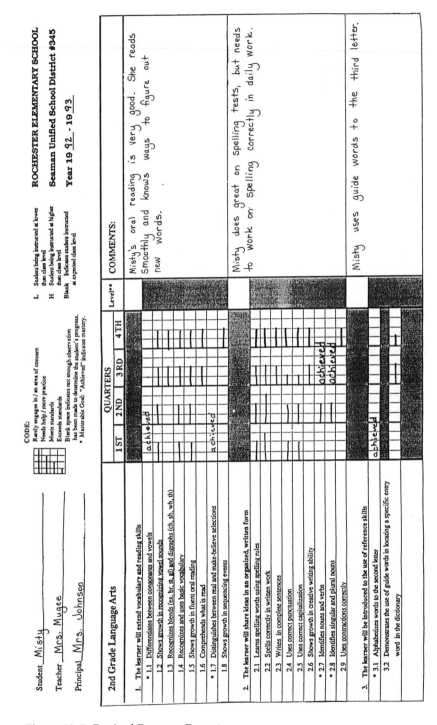

Figure 10–5 *Revised Progress Report*

Student Misty

Teacher Mrs. Mugee

Principal Mrs. Johnson

ROCHESTER ELEMENTARY SCHOOL

Seaman Unified School District #345

Year 19 92 - 19 93

CODE:

Rarely engages in / an area of concern

Needs help / more practice

Meets standards

Exceeds standards

Blank space indicates not enough observation has been made to determine the student's progress.

* Measurable Goal: "Achieved" indicates mastery.

L Student being instructed at lower than class level

H Student being instructed at higher than class level

Blank Indicates student instructed at expected class level

2nd Grade Language Arts

1. The learner will extend vocabulary and reading skills
   - • 1.1 Differentiates between consonants and vowels
   - 1.2 Shows growth in recognizing vowel sounds
   - 1.3 Recognizes blends (ex. br, st, gl) and digraphs (ch, sh, wh, th)
   - 1.4 Recognizes and uses basic vocabulary
   - 1.5 Shows growth in fluent oral reading
   - 1.6 Comprehends what is read
   - • 1.7 Distinguishes between real and make-believe selections
   - 1.8 Shows growth in sequencing events

2. The learner will share ideas in an organized, written form
   - 2.1 Learns spelling words using spelling rules
   - 2.2 Spells correctly in written work
   - 2.3 Writes in complete sentences
   - 2.4 Uses correct punctuation
   - 2.5 Uses correct capitalization
   - 2.6 Shows growth in creative writing ability
   - • 2.7 Identifies nouns and verbs
   - • 2.8 Identifies singular and plural nouns
   - 2.9 Uses contractions correctly

3. The learner will be introduced to the use of reference skills
   - • 3.1 Alphabetizes words to the second letter
   - 3.2 Demonstrates the use of guide words in locating a specific entry word in the dictionary

COMMENTS:

Misty's oral reading is very good. She reads smoothly and knows ways to figure out new words.

Misty does great on spelling tests, but needs to work on spelling correctly in daily work.

Misty uses guide words to the third letter.

Student: Misty

Teacher: Mrs. Mugee

Principal: Mrs. Johnson

ROCHESTER ELEMENTARY SCHOOL

Seaman Unified School District #345

Year 19 92 - 19 93

CODE:
⊞ Rarely engages in / is an area of concern
⊞ Needs help / more practice
⊞ Meets standards
⊞ Exceeds standards
Blank space indicates not enough observation has been made to determine the student's progress.
* Masterable Goal: "Achieved" indicates mastery.

LEVEL**
L Student being instructed at lower than class level
H Student being instructed at higher than class level
Blank Indicates student instructed at expected class level

COMMENTS: Misty has memorized her math facts, so she can solve problems quickly, and easily.

2nd Grade Math

	QUARTERS 1ST	2ND	3RD	4TH	Level**
1. The learner will show growth in computation skills					
* 1.1 Accurately uses addition and subtraction skills to 10					
* 1.2 Recalls addition facts through sums to 10		achieved			
* 1.3 Recalls subtraction facts related to sums through 10			achieved		
1.4 Accurately uses addition and subtraction skills to 18				achieved	
* 1.5 Recalls addition facts through sums to 18					
* 1.6 Recalls subtraction facts related to sums through 18					
1.7 Shows understanding of place value (ones, tens, and hundreds)					
1.8 Applies place value concepts to read and write 3 digit numbers			achieved		
1.9 Computes addition problems with up to 2 digit numbers using one trade			achieved		
* 1.10 Computes addition problems with up to 3 digit numbers using one to two trades			achieved		
* 1.11 Computes subtraction problems with up to 2 digit numbers using one trade				achieved	
* 1.12 Computes subtraction problems with up to 3 digit numbers using one to two trades				achieved	
1.13 Shows growth in skip-counting by twos, threes, fives, and tens					
1.14 Understands concepts of multiplication					
2. The learner will show growth in measurement skills					
* 2.1 Reads and writes times to the hour and half hour		achieved			
2.2 Shows growth in reading and writing time to five-minute intervals					
* 2.3 Accurately measures using centimeters and inches			achieved		
* 2.4 Recognizes and writes simple fractions					
3. The learner will show growth in money skills					
3.1 Recognizes and counts coins to $1.00					
4. The learner will show growth in problem-solving					
4.1 Shows growth in solving a one-step problem involving addition or subtraction				achieved	

Figure 10–5 (Continued)

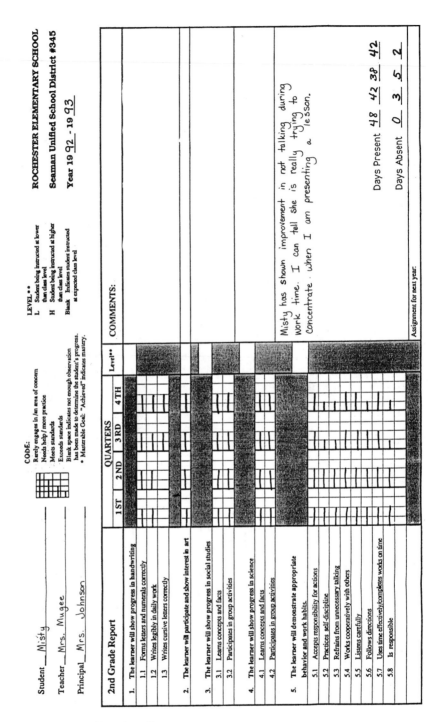

Figure 10–5 (Continued)

124

In May, the staff again asked the school board to continue the progress report and make changes to reflect district curriculum changes. Rubrics developed by the district would be used to increase consistency among teachers of the same grade level in assessing student work. Parents would continue to have opportunities to give formal responses. The board accepted the progress report, but asked for a yearly update.

The staff found the progress report to be very helpful in setting up an "at-risk" program. We designated certain competency levels on the report. At-risk students were identified at the beginning of the school year based on the final report from the previous year. These students were tutored on the specific objectives they did not complete the previous year. Students were added to the program and released based on the current progress report. The same approach was used to identify students for the summer school program. In both programs, four teachers worked with the students for half-hour intervals on specific objectives. If a student only needed one half-hour session, then that student attended only a half hour each day. The teachers set the schedule according to the students' needs.

YEAR FIVE

- Teachers revised objectives and coding.
- Staff continued the outcomes education process, using the progress report as an evaluation tool.
- Parent night was held during the first week of school.
- Teachers continued using the progress report to identify students for the at-risk program and summer school.
- Parents continued to be informed about teaching methods and non-letter-grade research through weekly school newsletter.
- Administrators and teachers were always available to answer questions concerning progress report.
- The progress report format was put on computer for use by all teachers.

Again, the objectives and coding were revised, based on the parent forum the previous year and concerns raised at the May school board meeting (see Figure 10–6). To address possible misinterpretation, the word *standards* was changed to *expectations*.

The progress report was also used for evaluation for the state assessment program. Teachers identified key areas in the curriculum that needed improvement. In-service was used to more fully develop teachers' knowledge and skills.

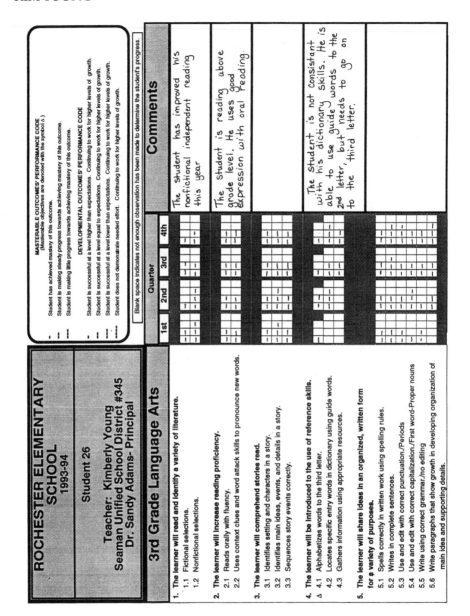

Figure 10–6 *Revised Progress Report, Rochester Elementary School 1993–94*

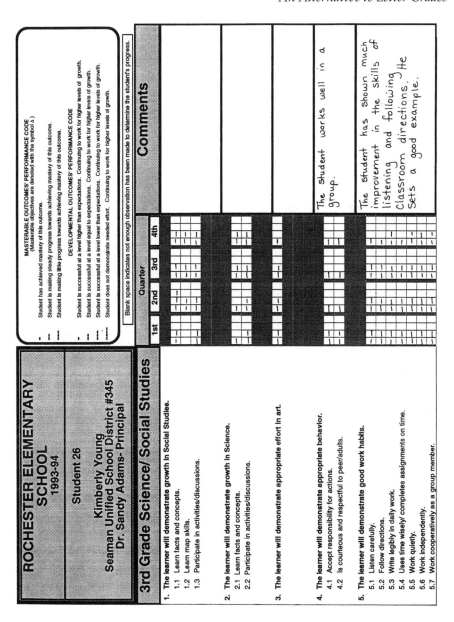

ROCHESTER ELEMENTARY SCHOOL
1993-94

Student 26

Kimberly Young
Seaman Unified School District #345
Dr. Sandy Adams- Principal

MASTERABLE OUTCOMES' PERFORMANCE CODE
(Masterable objectives are denoted with the symbol ▲)

⎯ Student has achieved mastery of this outcome.

-- Student is making steady progress towards achieving mastery of this outcome.

···· Student is making little progress towards achieving mastery of this outcome.

DEVELOPMENTAL OUTCOMES' PERFORMANCE CODE

⎯ Student is successful at a level higher than expectations. Continuing to work for higher levels of growth.

-- Student is successful at a level equal to expectations. Continuing to work for higher levels of growth.

···· Student is successful at a level lower than expectations. Continuing to work for higher levels of growth.

⎯⎯ Student does not demonstrate needed effort. Continuing to work for higher levels of growth.

Blank space indicates not enough observation has been made to determine the student's progress.

3rd Grade Science/ Social Studies

	Quarter				Comments
	1st	2nd	3rd	4th	
1. The learner will demonstrate growth in Social Studies.					
1.1 Learn facts and concepts.					
1.2 Learn map skills.					
1.3 Participate in activities/discussions.					
2. The learner will demonstrate growth in Science.					
2.1 Learn facts and concepts.					
2.2 Participate in activities/discussions.					
3. The learner will demonstrate appropriate effort in art.					
4. The learner will demonstrate appropriate behavior.					The student works well in a group.
4.1 Accept responsibility for actions.					
4.2 Is courteous and respectful to peer/adults.					
5. The learner will demonstrate good work habits.					The student has shown much improvement in the skills of listening and following classroom directions. He sets a good example.
5.1 Listen carefully.					
5.2 Follow directions.					
5.3 Write legibly in daily work.					
5.4 Uses time wisely/ completes assignments on time.					
5.5 Work quietly.					
5.6 Work independently.					
5.7 Work cooperatively as a group member.					

Figure 10–6 *(Continued)*

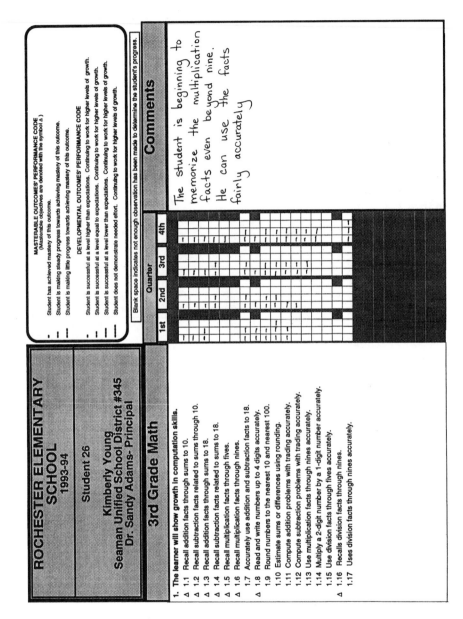

Figure 10–6 *(Continued)*

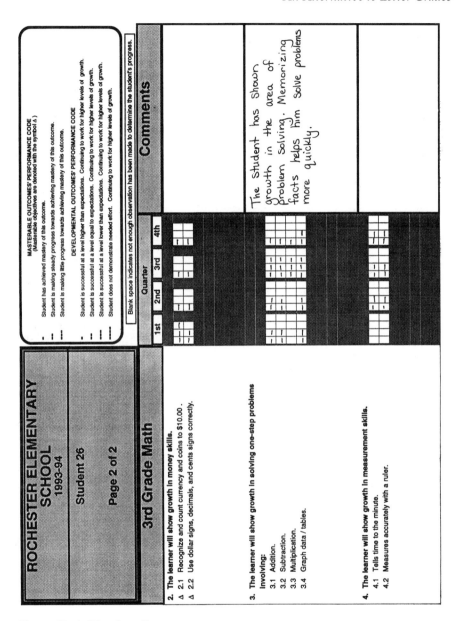

ROCHESTER ELEMENTARY SCHOOL
1993-94

Student 26

Page 2 of 2

3rd Grade Math

MASTERABLE OUTCOMES' PERFORMANCE CODE
(Masterable objectives are denoted with the symbol △.)

- Student has achieved mastery of this outcome.
-- Student is making steady progress towards achieving mastery of this outcome.
--- Student is making little progress towards achieving mastery of this outcome.

DEVELOPMENTAL OUTCOMES' PERFORMANCE CODE

- Student is successful at a level higher than expectations. Continuing to work for higher levels of growth.
-- Student is successful at a level equal to expectations. Continuing to work for higher levels of growth.
--- Student is successful at a level lower than expectations. Continuing to work for higher levels of growth.
---- Student does not demonstrate needed effort. Continuing to work for higher levels of growth.

Blank space indicates not enough observation has been made to determine the student's progress.

2. The learner will show growth in money skills.
△ 2.1 Recognize and count currency and coins to $10.00.
△ 2.2 Use dollar signs, decimals, and cents signs correctly.

3. The learner will show growth in solving one-step problems involving:
3.1 Addition.
3.2 Subtraction.
3.3 Multiplication.
3.4 Graph data / tables.

4. The learner will show growth in measurement skills.
4.1 Tells time to the minute.
4.2 Measures accurately with a ruler.

	Quarter			Comments
1st	2nd	3rd	4th	
				The student has shown growth in the area of problem solving. Memorizing facts helps him solve problems more quickly.

Figure 10–6 *(Continued)*

After completing the yearly revision, the staff continued to educate the community on the benefits of a nongraded reporting system. Today in the classroom, teachers focus on developing the most effective management techniques. The goal now is continued use of the progress report.

CONCLUSION

Based on its experience developing the progress report, the Rochester Elementary School faculty developed a list of suggestions for those considering a change in reporting systems:

- Include parents from the very beginning of the change process. Parents, like educators, will not accept change unless the need can be identified.
- Include the school board from the beginning of the process. Inform members of your intentions and proposals early. Do not try to make changes without their approval.
- Consider working into a nongraded report card one grade level at a time. Rochester teachers began the progress report with all grade levels in one year. The upper grade levels had difficulty adapting to the new evaluation system because the students had been receiving letter grades for one to three years.
- Teachers must develop new reporting systems because they are the people who will use them. The success of our progress report was due to the fact that 100 percent of the staff was included in the report's development and revision. A staff will accept and support change more easily if the change is developed from within. The staff's attendance at every board meeting at which the progress report was considered and at parent forums sent a clear message to the community about the staff's belief in and support of the system.

Our staff considers the progress report to be in continual revision. The report is constantly being updated and revised as part of a process of growth and development. There is no final product, only many drafts.

Chapter 11
Student, Parent, Teacher Collaboration

LISA BIETAU

Reporting student progress is an ongoing process involving parents, teachers, and students. This process includes continuous written and oral communication throughout the school year as well as formal meetings and written reports summarizing progress. The ultimate goal of collaboration among all stakeholders is to enhance student success. The more time and energy spent developing strong partnerships, the more effectively the classroom operates and students' needs are met. Successful partnerships depend on continuous communication and feedback from all partners. Such partnerships can be greatly enhanced through trust-building experiences, clarity of communications, and training for all stakeholders in thoughtful reflection and collaborative skills.

Traditional reporting systems rely primarily on the perspective of the classroom teacher. However, collaboration by parent, teacher, and students allows for multiple perspectives. To maximize these three distinct perspectives, participants must direct their conversations toward specific learner targets. These targets can be developed by the district, school, or classroom teachers. Clearly identifying specific learner targets enables both students and parents to participate in collecting evidence of students' growth. Therefore, the heart of collaboration is to focus on learner success as measured by progress toward accomplishing learner targets (see Figure 11–1).

When the responsibility of monitoring progress is shared by all stakeholders, more and better data are collected. Collecting evidence from three perspectives greatly enhances the validity of the student progress report. The conference becomes an opportunity for stakeholders to present their

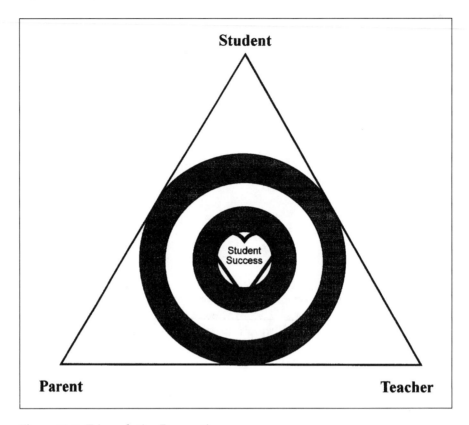

Figure 11–1 *Triangulating Perspectives*

evidence and look for patterns of behavior that document progress. This dialogue becomes the summary and analysis of student performance. The thoughtful reflection by triangulated partners during the conference is the essential component for continual improvement.

The collection of evidence that demonstrates growth toward learner targets is often referred to as "portfolio assessment." Portfolio assessment is a monitoring strategy that nurtures student self-assessment and builds on successes while enabling students to learn from mistakes. Portfolio assessment links teaching, assessment, and learning. Active learning experiences, which emphasize the process of learning, help ensure the process is valued as well as a final product.

A portfolio is an assessment strategy whereby evidence of a student's learning is systematically compiled by students and teachers. Parents may also contribute to this process. The exact purpose of the collection can range from celebrating achievement to monitoring progress toward learning objectives. The intended audience is typically the parent, student, and teacher, but can vary since this strategy also can be used to demonstrate accountability or qualifications for future opportunities.

Building portfolios is an exercise in research. Children are collecting evidence of their skills and knowledge as they perform a variety of tasks. Compiling this information from multiple perspectives enhances its accuracy.

Teachers lay the groundwork for portfolios during parent orientations about two weeks into the school year. During that time, teachers share their philosophy of education, background, and curricular map complete with learner targets for the year. Parents receive copies of the district outcomes, which are written as program goals on the elementary learning profile (Figure 11–2). At the parent orientation, parents are asked to think about their child's strengths and challenges as well as what makes them giggle and worry (Figure 11–3). All of these areas are to be discussed at the goal-setting conference the following week. The children are asked to complete the same form during class and then use this reflection as the basis for the first conversation at the goal-setting conference. During the parent orientation, individual after-school conferences are scheduled for every child and parent. If possible, goal-setting sessions can be held in the child's home. Home visits are extremely valuable, but difficult to manage owing to the travel time required. The purpose of the goal-setting conference is to set two personal goals. One goal is designed to build on the child's strength and the other to address an area of challenge or need. The conference begins with all team members presenting their perspectives using the sheet listing strengths, challenges, giggles, and worries. From this discussion, a collective list is compiled of strengths and challenges. Participants ask probing questions to clarify these examples. Then the partners are asked to advocate the goal they individually think is most important. The group then strives to prioritize its list to identify one goal of strength and one of challenge. These areas are listed on the goal-setting form, which becomes a part of the child's learning profile. This process gives parents and students a voice in designing two learning targets that are customized to meet individual needs both at school and home (see Figure 11–4).

The learning environment must reflect the expectations presented to parents. This will require adjustment of daily classroom routines. This is accomplished by allowing blocks of time for thematic teaching that guides students through a series of inquiry experiences. The design of the classroom is flexible and child centered, yet it keeps up-front the mission to

Expeditions

Exploring New Possibilities

Amanda Arnold Elementary Learning Profile

Student: Brad Artman   Age: 9
Teacher: Mrs. Bietau   Year: 94

Key: ☑	1	2	3	4	5
Not Assessed	Beginning	Improving	Getting There	Consistently Demonstrated/Mastery	Goes Beyond Expectations

Effective Communicator   ① II III IV

A. Demonstrates the ability to communicate in writing.

1. Demonstrates an understanding of the writing process.   [4][ ][ ][ ]

2. Demonstrates the ability to write for different purposes.   [4][ ][ ][ ]

3. Demonstrates application of the writing traits (analytical model) in writing:

   a. Idea/content   [4][ ][ ][ ]

   b. Organization   [3][ ][ ][ ]

   c. Voice/tone   [5][ ][ ][ ]

   d. Effective word choice   [5][ ][ ][ ]

   e. Sentence fluency   [4][ ][ ][ ]

   f. Writing conventions   [3][ ][ ][ ]

4. Organizes written communication (readable.)   [3][ ][ ][ ]

B. Demonstrates that reading is a process which varies with material, purpose, and reader.

1. Shows uses of different approaches based upon purpose, difficulty, and understanding.   [5][ ][ ][ ]

2. Shows understanding of material read.   [4][ ][ ][ ]

3. Shows a positive attitude towards reading.   [5][ ][ ][ ]

C. Demonstrates active listening skills.

1. Asks questions to extend and clarify learning.   [5][ ][ ][ ]

2. Participates in discussions.   [5][ ][ ][ ]

3. Follows a sequence of directions.   [3][ ][ ][ ]

Figure 11-2 *Expeditions—Amanda Arnold Elementary Learning Profile*

D. Demonstrates effective speaking skills. `4 □ □ □`

    1. Speaks loudly and clearly. `4 □ □ □`

    2. Presents points in logical order. `4 □ □ □`

    3. Interacts with audience. `4 □ □ □`

E. Demonstrates mastery of weekly spelling lists. `4 □ □ □`

Self-Directed Learner

A. Demonstrates a positive attitude towards learning.

    1. Eagerly accepts a challenge. `5 □ □ □`

    2. Demonstrates interest, curiosity, and inventiveness. `5 □ □ □`

B. Uses work time wisely.

    1. Makes responsible choices independently. `3 □ □ □`

    2. Plans, organizes and carries through a task to completion.

        a. Takes responsibility for completing homework. `4 □ □ □`

        b. Takes responsibility for completing assignments in school. `3 □ □ □`

        c. Can keep an organized work area. `4 □ □ □`

C. Monitors and evaluates progress. `4 □ □ □`

D. Demonstrates self-control. `3 □ □ □`

E. Manages information by demonstrating use of study and reference skills:

    1. Locates materials in LMC. `5 □ □ □`

    2. Uses a variety of reference materials, organizers, and picture aids. `5 □ □ □`

Quality Producer

A. Creates products using advanced technologies. `5 □ □ □`

B. Creates products which reflect high standards and originality. `5 □ □ □`

C. Expresses enjoyment after achievement. `5 □ □ □`

D. Knows how to use mathematical computations. `5 □ □ □`

Figure 11–2 *(Continued)*

Complex Thinker

A. Identifies and understands problems in different situations. ☑☐☐☐

B. Uses available information and resources. ☑☐☐☐

C. Demonstrates an understanding of the scientific processes. ☑☐☐☐

D. Effectively uses higher-order thinking skills. ☑☐☐☐

Community Contributor

A. Identifies and discusses local and global issues. ☑☐☐☐

B. Demonstrates an understanding of multiple cultures. ☑☐☐☐

C. Explores earth's regions. ☑☐☐☐

D. Investigates human/environmental interactions. ☑☐☐☐

E. Contributes time and talents to local and/or global efforts to improve welfare of others. ☑☐☐☐

Collaborative Worker

A. Cooperates with others. ☑☐☐☐

B. Contributes to group work. ☑☐☐☐

C. Appreciates the value of diversity in others. ☑☐☐☐

D. Respects the rights and properties of others. ☑☐☐☐

Figure 11–2 *(Continued)*

make progress toward learner outcomes and personal goals. For example, at the beginning of the year, students work in cooperative groups to clarify the six learner outcomes and rewrite them in student language (Figure 11–5). These student-written outcomes become the operating document around which the classroom is designed.

As the quarter progresses, the class monitors daily activities and records connections to the targeted goals. Often the students see the connections to the targeted outcomes from a different perspective from that of the teacher who designed the activity. Including the student in the design of activities and criteria for evaluation usually results in high-quality products and effective process skills.

The following is a description of my experience assessing and reporting one student's progress. Brad is a fourth-grade student in a multi-age classroom. To complete a fourth-grade learner profile to share with Brad's parents at the end of the first quarter, I plan to monitor his progress toward

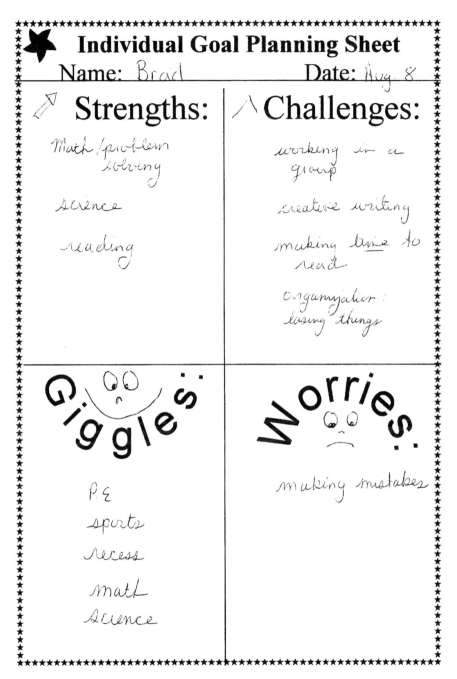

Individual Goal Planning Sheet

Name: Brad   Date: Aug. 8

Strengths:

Math/problem
        solving

science

reading

Challenges:

working in a
        group

creative writing

making time to
        read

organization:
losing things

Giggles:

P.E
sports
recess
math
science

Worries:

making mistakes

Figure 11–3 *Individual Goal Planning Sheet*

Personal Goal 1993-94

Student: Brad Rawlins
Date: Oct. 1993
Tr. Lisa Bietau

Goal : Building on student strength
To continue to develop math problem solving skills.
Plan...
Collect advanced problem solving experiences
Complete a Problem of the Week
Work on KATM math packet
Compete in the KATM Math Contest
Complete Math Packets from Grade 6 book
Comments:

Goal: Addressing a Challenge area
Learning to plan and complete a research project.
Plan...
Research "Wolf Creek Nuclear Plant"
Design a plan to complete the project by
Dec. 23.
Evaluate project and plan to complete it
Deomonstrate organizational skill
(Clean desk...Homework Tracker... Make Deadlines)
 Routinely Demonstrate Quality Work.
(Evaluate: 1—-3 Meets Requirements__5 Exceeds Req.)
Comments:

Figure 11–4 *Goal Setting Form*

**Student Created Descriptors
for District Outcomes**

Complex Thinker

If I am a complex thinker I would show evidence of thinking through complex problems. Some of the things I can do as a complex thinker are:

- Take my time when I approach a problem.
- Think hard about the problem (restate it in my own words).
- Use my time wisely to solve the problem.
- Be open-minded when brainstorming.
- Be a good listener.
- Look for more than one answer to the problem.

Quality Producer

I am a quality producer if I strive to go beyond the expectations of the task I am required to do. Some of the things I would do as a quality producer are:

- Use time well from the start to make it my best.
- Make sure my work is neat and organized.
- Feel good when the job is done knowing it is a job well done.
- Know the criteria for success on the project and that my work is of high standards; it is beyond what is expected.
- Revise work until high quality is met.
- Be creative in projects where it is expected.
- Show obvious craftsmanship through the use of tools (ie. use rulers to make lines for lettering).

Collaborative Worker

I am a collaborative worker who can work with other people to get a task done. Collaborative workers become partners where all members gain from the group. In other words, if well done it should be better than doing it yourself. (If you feel that you are doing it all then you are not collaborating, you are rescuing your teammates!) Some of the things I would do as a collaborative worker are:

- Cooperate as part of a team.
- Be aware of others and honor their needs.
- Work effectively in the partnership so that everyone contributes.
- Demonstrate self-control by using a quiet voice and staying on tasks.
- Be responsible; get the job done!
- Stay on task.
- Use encouraging words.
- Demonstrate cooperative audience skills.
- Listen to team members.
- Divide the responsibility so that all members have a chance to contribute! (No hogging work!)
- Use the talents of the goup; match talent to the task!

Figure 11–5 *Student Created Descriptors for District Outcomes*

Effective Communicator

I communicate clearly so that others understand my message or spoken words. I am able to understand other people's ideas by reading or listening. I ask questions until the message is understood by the audience. As an effective communicator, I can:

- Use neat handwriting that is easy to read.
- Speak ideas in a clear and organized way so that I am understood.
- Listen while others express their ideas.
- Respond to another person's ideas in a way that they know I understand.
- Listen with an open mind; allow the ideas of others to change my own opinions or views.
- Read writing so that I can understand the author's message.
- React to the ideas I am hearing or reading by relating them to my own ideas and experiences.

Self-Directed Learner

As a self-directed learner, I am able to find out what needs to be done and find a way to do it. I understand the problem or task that is given and the resources available. I continue to work at the task or problem in a logical way until it is complete. As a self-directed learner, I can:

- Listen and question until I understand the task or problem I have been given.
- Locate and use resources available to me.
- Keep my work in progress organized and safe.
- Consider quality as I complete a task.
- Use complex thinking as a way to solve problems that occur on the way.
- Use mistakes as learning opportunities.
- Work independently with little repeating.
- Use coaches when I am stuck.
- Know how to set goals and achieve them.

Community Contributor

A community is a group of people collaborating together. These people cooperate by giving their talents and energy to the group so that the group can be successful. Communities may be your team, school, state, nation, or world. A community contributor gives back to the community in which he or she lives. As a community contributor, I can:

- Donate my extra time or talents to the group because they need me.
- Assist someone in the group who is having trouble.
- Focus on the community's needs (Act accordingly!).
- Try to improve the community by finding better ways for the community to operate.

Figure 11–5 *(Continued)*

both content and process outcomes as he researches, summarizes, and works to complete his assignments. I keep several records of his progress. Each assignment focuses on attributes of the learner outcomes. The compilation of various learning experiences and projects offers a complete assessment of Brad's progress toward the outcomes. For example, Figure 11–6 features a math problem of the week that focuses on three of the learner

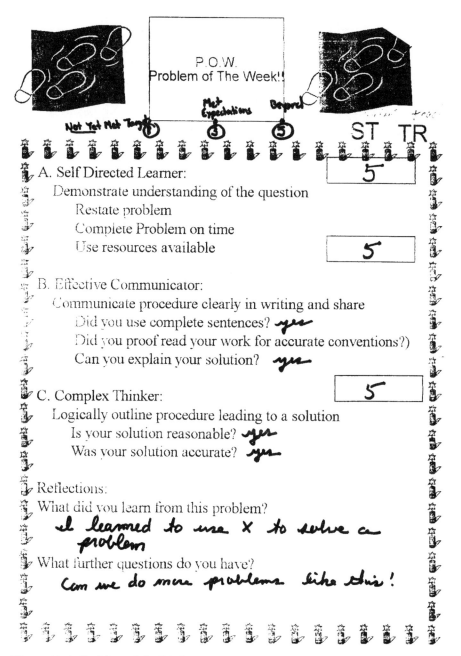

P.O.W.
Problem of The Week!!

Met Expectations   Beyond

Not Yet Not Taught

ST   TR

5

A. Self Directed Learner:
    Demonstrate understanding of the question
        Restate problem
        Complete Problem on time
        Use resources available

5

B. Effective Communicator:
    Communicate procedure clearly in writing and share
        Did you use complete sentences? *yes*
        Did you proof read your work for accurate conventions?)
        Can you explain your solution? *yes*

5

C. Complex Thinker:
    Logically outline procedure leading to a solution
        Is your solution reasonable? *yes*
        Was your solution accurate? *yes*

Reflections:
What did you learn from this problem?
    I learned to use X to solve a problem
What further questions do you have?
    Can we do more problems like this!

Figure 11–6 *Problem of the Week*

outcomes. These P.O.W.'s are collected and evaluated by the student (ST) and Teacher (TR) each week. They are kept in the student's portfolio as part of the evidence of progress in complex thinking, self-directed learning, and effective communicating which will be used later to complete the learner profile.

As Brad's teacher, I monitor his progress on both content and process outcomes as he researches, summarizes, and works to complete his Canadian history assignment. I keep several records of his progress during this six-week study. I monitor his daily work habits, looking at summarizing, communicating ideas effectively, research skills, and productivity. My feedback and observations are recorded and continually shared with Brad. A summary of my observations is applied to the criteria sheet at the end of the project (Figure 11–7). I note that Brad was unable to locate information relating to his selected topic on the computer card catalogue, so he referenced books on Canadian history and used the index successfully to get started on his research. This qualifies as an example of how Brad "considered a variety of alternatives when solving a problem."

When facilitating an independent inquiry in my classroom, the children set individual research goals and a plan to accomplish this in the given time. At the end of our research time, Brad reflects on his progress (see Figure 11–8). This is where Brad notes his frustration and his solution. He knows that recording the details of a problem-solving situation is valued in our class. At the end of each session, there is a five-minute wrap-up, during which the kids record what they've accomplished. A five-minute discussion follows, during which we share accomplishments and frustrations. I then can make plans to attend to those in need and make suggestions aloud that apply to more than one situation. Brad's use of the index may sound trivial, but many students forget this trick and sit frustrated with nothing to do until an adult intervenes. The short discussion focusing on the process and problem solving used that day allows many students to benefit from Brad's learning experience.

This portfolio assessment strategy is only accurate if the culture of learning in the classroom allows learning opportunities to be extended and teaches prerequisite skills needed to be successful. For example, Brad should be provided access to the library and appropriate technology and other resources as needed. My classroom should offer Brad multiple opportunities to demonstrate this type of learning by creating a culture that promotes inquiry and builds prerequisite skills.

Standards for each content and process outcome are explained and published at the beginning of each assignment. With these criteria established early on, the students are invited to exceed or extend beyond the requirements. Never placing a ceiling on performance makes the opportunity to

NAME_____

SUCCESS CRITERIA

CANADA ADVENTURE I
A TRIP THROUGH HISTORY

Using the following scale rate your success for work completed on your Canada history project.

1   3   5

score of 1 - criteria requirements have not yet been met
score of 3 - criteria requirements met
score of 5 - criteria requirements met and are above expectations

	ST	TR
EFFECTIVE COMMUNICATOR		
Ideas in summary are clearly organized		
Ideas in illustration are clearly organized		
Proper Conventions		
SELF-DIRECTED LEARNER		
Project completed on time		
Time was used wisely		
Considered a variety of alternatives when solving a problem		
COMPLEX THINKER		
Does project summarize the main ideas about the time in Canadian history?		
QUALITY PRODUCER		
Craftsmanship		
Creative Layout		
Creative Ideas		

Student Comments:

Teacher Comments:

Figure 11–7 *Criteria Sheet*

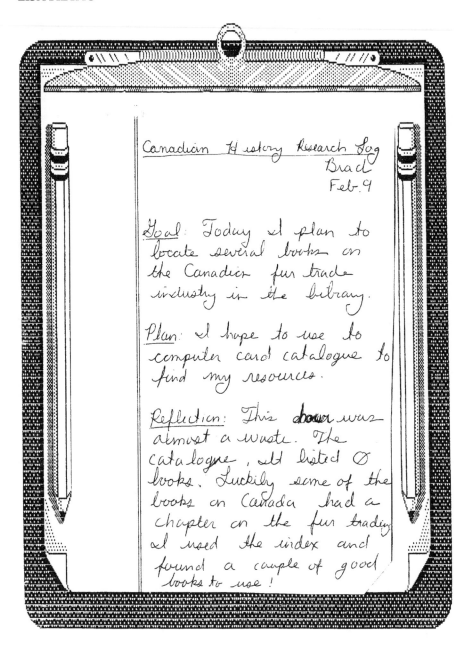

Figure 11–8 *Research Log*

go beyond continually available and students extend themselves intentionally. This creates an expectation to go beyond whenever possible. These open-ended activities can be adapted to all learning styles and abilities so all learners are considered and valued. They allow for both process skills and product qualities to be assessed. Brad's parents are given the criteria for success up-front and can begin their observations of his performance on these assignments immediately. If the criteria are unclear to Brad or his parents, they have the chance to clear up any confusion by writing a note on the criteria sheet that requires a parent's signature. The continual refinement of criteria is essential to keep communication clear among partners.

Parents should be encouraged to be reflective and should be invited to provide input about the portfolio collection. This can be accomplished by including them in the ongoing evaluation process. The more clearly the criteria are communicated, the more comfortable parents will feel giving feedback. They need opportunities to praise the child's performance or efforts as well as to "nudge" when there are areas that can be improved. Keeping a section for comments allows parents to offer their summary perspectives. It also provides a place for comments that are not listed in the targeted criteria but that may be significant to the student's performance.

Communication must be ongoing among the partners. Weekly newsletters are an efficient strategy to keep parents informed of past, present, and future events. Newsletters can be attached to criteria sheets and project overviews that relate to the week's agenda. Newsletters and calendars can become a planning and recording device for the partners, and should be sent home regularly. Work assessed the previous week can also be sent home for parents' review and evaluation. This evidence should then be returned to the teacher for placement in the student's portfolio. Weekly communication deepens parents' involvement and often promotes discussions between parent and child regarding school goals, outcomes, and weekly performance. Telephone calls also give partners quick access to information.

Although conferences are scheduled quarterly, partners may call the team together whenever concerns arise. Quarterly conferences include twenty to thirty minutes to report data and look for patterns of improvement or concern. Although the opportunity for face-to-face conferences is always available to my students and their parents, the quarterly meeting is dedicated to celebrating growth through study of the evidence presented.

Quarterly conferences replace the two traditional fall and spring meetings of the past. Students are always present at the conferences and are given key roles in presenting the evidence gathered during the quarter.

Because the quarterly conference differs from the typical teacher-led conference, it requires planning and the establishment of new roles for the teacher, parent, and student. In the past, parents listened to a report by the teacher summarizing their child's progress. The child did not participate in the conversation. A "collaborative conference" changes the teacher's role to that of facilitator while parent and student share their data. Sharing is complete when the teacher presents collected data. Together the partners look for growth and areas that need further attention.

Students need to be taught how to present their data in a concise, effective way. I encourage students to practice ahead of time with other students who play the role of parents. This is fun and is crucial to easing students' anxiety. Older students who have experience with the process can guide and coach younger children. Displaying a video tape of an actual conference is a helpful way to begin. Then students can demonstrate the process by role-playing the teacher, parent, and student.

This practice is essential for enabling students to make an organized presentation at the conference. The students rehearse using audible voices, making eye contact, and practicing other effective communication behaviors. Students also complete a form outlining the comments they wish to make during the conference.

Students then select significant pieces of work to be tagged with reflections and comments regarding why they felt these pieces were special. Brad included his reading log as evidence of self-directed learning because he read without being asked. I encouraged Brad to find an entry for each of the six learner outcomes and two additional entries for what we call "just because" (work selected simply because he liked it) and "O.O.P.S.!" (Outstanding Opportunity for a Personal Stretch!).

As a teacher, I must summarize my thoughts and outline crucial evidence for each child, and I must present this information in a ten minute time span. This causes me to prioritize and customize my presentation for each child. Keeping to the time limit is difficult but necessary. Further conference dates or follow-up phone calls can be made to share information the adults are not comfortable sharing in front of the student.

At the first quarter conference, Brad's evidence of self-directed learning shows a pattern of outstanding research skills and effort, but work is needed in completing the assignment on time. The group suggests that Brad apply the strategy of planning backwards from the due date and breaking the task into smaller pieces, which would allow for a quality performance to be accomplished on time. This was targeted as an area of personal challenge and prioritized as a goal for the next quarter. Often the conference includes a mini-lesson during which the teacher actually conducts a performance task or elaboration of a concept the student is working on while the parents watch. This helps to teach parents how to promote this concept at home.

A summary of student progress is recorded on the learner profile that is outlined according to district learner outcomes. The student and teacher fill these forms out separately and then compare their conclusions. Any discrepancies are discussed until a consensus is reached. The patterns of behavior and/or performance are documented and sent to the parents and school office for the permanent record of progress.

At the end of the second quarter, I usually design a more flexible confer-ence with a demonstration-and-sharing format. The "share fair" open house allows parents to see and experience the learning in action and to ac-tually interact with their child in the learning environment. This visit typi-cally lasts thirty minutes to an hour for each family, although the entire event may take three hours. The class sets up stations for parents and stu-dents to participate in interactive experiences that focus on targeted learner outcomes. Brad takes his parents to as many stations as he feels time al-lows. Student portfolios and a ten-minute personal goal conference with the teacher are mandatory stations. The purpose of this brief meeting is to discuss progress toward personal goals. Additions, deletions, or concerns may be presented at this time, as well as evidence collected from the group showing growth toward the goal.

The second-quarter learner profile is sent home prior to this conference, and parents are invited to set up private conferences to discuss their child's progress in greater detail if needed. The opportunity to discuss marks or suggest revisions is always a parent's option. About four or five families are scheduled each hour, and the school is open from 5 P.M. to 9 P.M. The stu-dents have prepared activities to share with their parents and they rehearse with a "study buddy," or student partner. The room is arranged to facilitate the flow of traffic. Some desks are removed to the hallway and a semipri-vate area set up to discuss personal goals with the teacher. Parents are invited to make observations on their child's performance of tasks demon-strated at the stations. Brad's parents note that he had difficulty explaining the concept of division using cubes at the math table. He was encouraged to continue to work with these manipulatives at home and school and try again at the third-quarter meeting. A meeting will be scheduled earlier if needed!

Third-quarter progress reports are sent home prior to a thirty-minute "collaborative conference" that follows the same format as the first quar-ter's. Children again practice preparing to lead the conference. Conver-sations during these conferences are always stimulating, enlightening, and productive. By the time of this conference, the team has established rap-port and is more at ease and more honest. If the conference environment has remained safe and each member, including the student, feels protected from attack, then the third-quarter conference can be the most productive.

The "celebration of learning" is held at the end of the fourth quarter. This whole-group gathering is designed to share evidence with the learning community that has been developed throughout the year. We often have a whole-group performance in the gym and then return to the room for the stations and portfolio review. Conferencing with the teacher is optional. A schedule is posted on the front chalkboard for those wishing a thirty-minute private conference on this Saturday morning.

This event represents the efforts of a teaching team of four classrooms, so planning it has been quite interesting. We use the hallways, lobby, computer lab, and library to accommodate the crowd. When planning this for a single classroom, I would schedule the whole-group presentation in the gym and then divide the crowd into two groups. One group would have refreshments while the other began the room tour. All students had a number. The even-numbered kids went for refreshments while the odd-numbered students visited the room stations. Once a group had completed its task, it moved to the alternate activity. This helped to manage the crowd and gave a loose structure to the evening. But the team approach is my personal favorite because all students are there together. The energy level escalates as we pull together to demonstrate growth and celebrate the year's highlights. We usually have one outstanding group project each year, which gives all class members the satisfaction of being part of something truly special. Many students don't have this feeling about their work as often as they should.

All students have carefully prepared their "celebration portfolios" by selecting tagged items from each of the four quarters. The tagged items, which each include a thoughtful response from the selecting person (parent, teacher, or child), are assembled with a table of contents in a folded envelope made of tagboard. It is freely decorated and secured with a Velcro seal. Brad's letter of reflection invites viewers to notice certain pieces or patterns (see Figure 11–9). This is shared with the family. The evidence that is not tagged is also released to parents; only the celebration portfolio is to be kept for next year's teacher to review.

Individual fourth-quarter conferences are held the Saturday after the school year ends and are targeted at setting summer goals. These conferences are optional but meet the needs of parents who want time to analyze progress made throughout the year. The individual fourth-quarter conference may be used to make final placement decisions for the next year.

Brad's cumulative record is updated with a copy of his "learner profile," including the progress he made toward his personal goals. A short

June 2, 1994

Dear Reader,

Hi! My name is Brad and I'm a fourth grade student at Amanda Arnold Elementary school. In my spare time I enjoy baseball, football, and basketball. I collect sports cards in these three sports.

As you look at my portfolio I'd like you to notice these things about my work... craftsmanship, creativity and complex thinking. My conservation poster is a great example of my artistic ability and creativity. History Day research led me to a quality product as I completed a model of the "Soo Lock" of Michigan accompanied by a display of how locks help connect the St. Lawrence Seaway. My evidence of complex thinking can be found in my math "Problem of the Week" folder. My explanation of the problem, procedure and solution can all be found in this folder.

Figure 11–9 *Letter of Reflection*

Looking back over the year I learned that organization is very important if you want to get the job done on time. Working in a group is hard, but I like it. I guess challenges are good even if you don't feel like doing it!

Make sure you look at my interview with a field biologist. This was my career report and I loved spending time with a real scientist. I still hope to be a scientist some day.

I hope you'll enjoy looking at my work!

Sincerely,
Brad Artman

P.S. My favorite Writers Workshop story is "My Hero". If you have time please read it!

Figure 11-9 *(Continued)*

narrative commenting on this progress, a sample from his writing portfolio, and his reading log are also included. A cover letter explaining the alternative reporting system accompanies the report so that if he moves to a new location they understand how to interpret the alternative assessment report.

COLLABORATIVE CHALLENGES

The use of technology in writing the narratives, designing assessments, and publishing newsletters is essential to save time. Computers in my home and at school give me access to the tools needed to maintain communication. We work very hard to see that all teachers have access to and the skill to use this technology.

Time is a fixed resource. There are only twenty-four hours in a day, and our career and family responsibilities demand much of us in this short amount of time. Collaborative conferences require that time be dedicated toward accomplishing the partnership. This means that some other activity may have to be abandoned to balance the equation of life. I found that I was unable to continue managing "book club" orders. I was fortunate to find a parent volunteer to manage the project. Fewer learner targets are focused on each quarter, but our community of learners seems to demonstrate a better understanding for what we do explore ("Less is More!"). My criteria for "beautiful bulletin boards" changed as the need for display areas for student work and informative posters replaced my artful ideas. The clutter around my room is a little deeper than it used to be, with projects in process often difficult to store. We do take photos of completed large projects so that after the quarter demonstration they may be taken home.

The process of nurturing and managing the partnership requires attention. Teachers must be aware at all times of the purpose of a meeting and carefully select a design that will accomplish that purpose. Feedback about a meeting's effectiveness will help to improve these strategies. The options explored in this chapter may be combined. For example, a staggered schedule, during which a teacher limits the time in the classroom to thirty minutes, is an option. Fifteen minutes are facilitated by the student and fifteen are spent with the collaborative partners. This means two conferences are going on simultaneously in different parts of the room. The teacher decides the purpose of the conference, then assembles the stakeholders and arranges the format. The method (or facilitator) and process for accomplishing the task are then decided.

Parent, Student, Teacher Conferences

Post Conference Reflection:

Date: _Oct. 30, 1994_

What do you value most about the scheduled conferences?

I enjoyed hearing Brad explain the classroom learning targets. As he summarized his learning we understood his performance level by viewing his work!

If you could change one thing about this conference what would it be?

It seemed like my son's teacher was given less opportunity to talk. Perhaps more time is needed with this format.

Was the purpose of this conference clear?

Yes! We were monitoring my son's progress quarterly on the outlined learning targets as well as personal goals.

Do you feel this purpose was accomplished?

Yes! We did take the portfolio home after the conference to view again.

Other Comments or Concerns:

I would like to meet again in four weeks to monitor Brad's personal goal of organization. Please let us know a good time for this.

Figure 11–10 *Parent, Student, Teacher Conference*

The group's operation must be held to a high standard. Setting and maintaining a few ground rules will enhance the relationships among partners:

- Start and stop on time.
- Display courtesy and respect.
- Have a good sense of humor.
- Disagree agreeably!
- Take care of personal needs.
- Listen actively; avoid side conversations.
- Contribute to personal and professional sharing opportunities.

Brief written or oral comments by participants on the effectiveness of the process at the close of each group meeting will help to build and maintain productive behavior (see Figure 11–10). Keep in mind that probing questions help to clarify ideas brought to the conference table and pausing allows for equal participation. Use active listening and paraphrasing to ensure that everyone understands. These skills can be taught and modeled in the classroom. Parents will learn from their children and from the modeled behavior at the conference.

Collaborative conferencing has benefits for all stakeholders. However, students especially have the opportunity to practice an essential life skill. When collaboration is practiced in a meaningful context, and dedicated to enhanced student progress, it is well worth the time, effort, and energy required.

REFERENCES

Anthony, R., T. Johnson, N. Mickelson & A. Preece. 1991. *Evaluating Literacy: A Perspective for Change*. Portsmouth, NH: Heinemann.

Bietau, L., J. Crill, & B. Maughmer. The Manhattan Assessment Project. *Student Portfolios*. Washington, D.C.: NEA Publications, 19–30.

Maughmer, B., L. Bietau, & J. Crill. 1993. "Assessing a Community of Learners: Authentic Assessment in Action." *Kansas ASCD Record* 11 (2):53–64.

Chapter 12
A Math/Science Perspective

RICHARD DRIVER

T hroughout public school, college, and graduate school, most of what I learned or was able to perform with respect to a course or subject was reduced to a single grade or number. For example, though I studied a number of topics in third-grade social studies, including the main exports of China and the characteristics of people in India, when all was said and done, my parents received a report of "B," or "89." They couldn't really tell, based on my report card, if I *knew* what the main exports of China were, and for the most part, didn't really care—only as long as I received a "good grade."

When my own two children were going through school, my chief concern as a parent was that they receive mostly "good grades," or that they perform "better than most of the others." I remember the time my son admitted to me that he had flunked an Algebra 2 test; my immediate question was "How did most of the others in your class do?" What was important was that he not be one of just a few who had "flunked." If most of the class had not mastered the material, then I could hold the Algebra 2 teacher accountable also.

Consider a second scenario: Your boss has just commended you for a job well done and points out in her secretary-typed note to you that you are "one of our company's valuable employees, etc., etc." But nothing specific about your work behavior, actions, or products is noted. You might well be wondering exactly *what* work your boss is referring to.

Consider how much more we like the note that says, "Marilee's office management skills are exemplary. She has successfully completed the reorganization of the filing system, making things much easier to find for all of us, and has so improved the bookkeeping operation that now she is able to report transactions and balances for each of our six general fund accounts and five grants monthly."

Consider a time in your own life when the praise you received was so generic as to be almost ineffective. One year, everything that was typed on my teacher evaluation form was, "Mr. Driver is a master teacher." I remember asking my principal in our short conference, "How can you say that—you have hardly been in my room?" I would have felt better about that short report, I believe, had there been a list of specific instances to document my "master teacher" status.

All of this is to point out that a report of progress reduced to a single letter or number does not usually tell all that should be told regarding someone's progress (or lack thereof). On the other hand, if the grade is "high" (and most of us know what that means), we have few questions; we conclude that the student learned and mastered what was taught and tested, and most of the time we are satisfied. But still the questions nag: *What* does the student know? What can the student *do*? And we can't answer based on a single letter or number.

The *Curriculum and Evaluation Standards for School Mathematics*, published by the National Council of Teachers of Mathematics (Reston, VA: NCTM, 1989), set the stage for a paradigm shift in the mathematics curriculum, of what is taught and what is learned. The shift was to a much richer content, with increased focus on *understanding* mathematics, and a reduced emphasis on computation as the end-product of elementary mathematics. This is not to say that computation is not important in elementary (or any other level of) mathematics, but it should not be the pinnacle, or focus, of all of curriculum and instruction at that level.

Briefly, the four themes of the NCTM's *Standards* are problem solving, communication, reasoning, and connections. At the very least we should report how students are progressing with regard to each of these themes. So perhaps the third-grade report card should have "mathematics" subdivided as follows:

Problem Solving: 82%
Communication: 86%
Reasoning: 66%
Connections: 90%

Had I needed to report all of this twenty-five years ago, I would probably have been tempted to find the arithmetic mean of these four numbers and just report "Mathematics: 81%." Or, I might have determined that some themes should have more weight than others and come up with a different, but (from my standpoint) defensible single number, somewhere between 66 and 90 percent.

Still, even with four grade components, the report is not complete. We still do not know what the student knows and does not know. We do not know what she can do and not do. We could prepare a multipage report on each student, complete with samples of work, teacher assessment and comments, and student self-assessment. We could even create a CD-ROM disk for each student that would include all of the above and much more, such as quick-time movies of the student *performing* mathematics!

The state of Kansas began statewide assessment of student performance in the fourth, seventh, and tenth grades several years ago based on these major themes and using three or four open-ended problems. This assessment has proven to be time-intensive for students, teachers, and the state assessment group. The assessment rubric for each item at each of the three grade levels reduces the assessment of a student's performance to an overall score of 0–5 and for some items scores for process skills (they include understanding the problem, choosing a problem-solving strategy, implementing a problem-solving strategy, and finding and reporting the solution). There is some move to drop the process skills assessment and report only the overall score to reduce scoring time and effort.

THE DILEMMA: EFFICIENCY OR COMPLETENESS?

The dilemma may lie in achieving a balance, based on the time and effort required, between assessment and reporting schemes that are efficient, and reduce assessment to a single number for reporting purposes (the traditional end-of-subject grade), and those that are authentic and integral to instruction, and evaluate and report the student's work in such a way as to preserve the essence of what the student knows and can do.

We must all ask ourselves, "Is it worth it?" If we truly believe that it is, then we must get on with the task of devising assessment that truly measures what we determine to be important, and then to report it in sufficient detail that interested parties will know what the student knows and can do. The Mathematical Sciences Education Board (MSEB) of the National Research Council published a book entitled *Measuring What Counts* (Washington, D.C. 1993). For purposes of this chapter, we might subtitle it "*Reporting* What Counts." Let us agree that it *is* worth it, and we *should* report what counts.

ASSESSING WHAT COUNTS

More than once I have stressed, in the teaching and learning of science, that "you aren't doing science if your hands aren't dirty!" In a slightly modified way, I believe the same goes for mathematics—what a student can do in mathematics is just as important as what she knows. We've said that before, but this time let's mean it; let's design assessments that get at both knowledge (facts) and performance, and then report this in meaningful ways.

Consider the following test question:

Find the perimeter for the given figure.

a. 10 m
b. 13 m
c. 26 m
d. 40 m

5 m

8 m

What can we conclude if students correctly mark answer "c" for this item? Can we be sure they know the definition of *perimeter* and can apply it to a rectangle?

Consider the following alternate form:

Draw a rectangle with a perimeter of 26 meters. Label the sides of the rectangle.

Now, it is argued, we can find out both what students *know* about perimeter of rectangles and what they are able to *perform* (they can draw a rectangle that satisfies the conditions). Notice also that there is now more than one correct answer. (In fact, there are infinite correct answers, but we'll not expect that of most students in the seventh grade!) The scorer of this alternate form of the item must know much more than to score the first item.

And, appropriately trained to score items like the alternate item, the teacher would then be able to "report what counts" regarding a student's knowledge and performance.

REPORTING WHAT COUNTS

Who will determine what the expectations are for performance assessments? Who better than appropriately trained staffs at the school district level. And who should devise the report card (perhaps more a *progress report*)? Obviously, no one person. A committee, including classroom teachers, district-level curriculum directors, principals, and parents should do it. The work of the committee must begin with in-service, as needed, to ensure that all members make the paradigm shift from traditional assessment and report of knowledge (reduced to a single letter or number) to a combination of knowledge and performance. As mentioned above, if the group wants students to understand perimeter of rectangles, it needs to understand that students must become invested in perimeters of rectangles, must draw some of their own, and probably measure dimensions of actual rooms, boxes, and so forth. Simply marking a, b, c, or d will not reveal what the student *knows* or doesn't know, and certainly does not reveal what the student can or cannot *do*.

To *know* mathematics is to *do* mathematics. Students will not become mathematically powerful simply because they can recite the multiplication tables or define *perimeter*. Students become powerful when they can do something with this knowledge, can put it to use in their own context. Recall the student who had worked making change in school, but was unable to make change when purchasing candy. The parent said, "But you learned how to make change—Mrs. Jones said you did." "No, that was in school," the student replied. For this student, what had been learned in school did not apply in real life.

Following are some items to consider in devising a progress report for mathematics:

- Balance the report between the student's knowledge and performance. Recognize that it is necessary to know certain things but more important to be able to do something with that knowledge.
- Agree on what is important to report. The report should not be so large as to be unwieldy and not used by teacher or parent. It is probably better to agree on a few significant performance skills and devise a report

that gives a rich description of the student's performance regarding these skills.

- Stick to specifics. The fact that "Jason is a good problem solver" is nice for a parent to know, but what does it mean?
- Avoid words and conventions that are ambiguous, too general, or smell of "educationese." It might impress parents to use educational terms, but it is not generally helpful.
- Consider a mixture of visual and verbal. Graphs are easy to generate with computers. Remember the adage, "a picture is worth a thousand words"? Sometimes it is!
- Summary letters and/or numbers (grades, percents, etc.) are not inherently bad, but use them in conjunction with other verbal and visual reporting.
- Consider using checklists for the "knowledge" aspects of the progress report. If a student *knows* the multiplication facts (hardly ever makes an error) and having this knowledge is one of the outcomes that is worthy both of assessment and report, then perhaps making a check in the box is all that is needed.

Knows Multiplication
Facts to 10×10

☐ Most of the time
☐ Emerging
☐ Not yet

- Consider ways to include student products in the report. This is easier when the report is discussed in the context of a parent-teacher conference. Then a student's portfolio can be the "show and tell" that documents the progress report.
- Consider inviting parents to "report day," when students give reports, demonstrations, and/or presentations about an assigned mathematical investigation. Involve students and parents in a rubric for assessing such reports so there are no secrets as to what is expected on a report.
- Devise a progress report that has meaning for students as well as for parents. (We say that we test that which is important. How about: "We *report* that which is important." If students see that "how well students apply the concept of perimeter to situations of their own making" is being reported, they have more reason to invest in it.)

AN EXAMPLE OF REPORTING WHAT
COUNTS IN MATHEMATICS, AND
THE CONCOMITANT DILEMMA

What follows is an example of a progress report for third-grade mathematics. This example represents not a well thought-out, finished product but rather, *a point of departure*.

I started with a curriculum guide listing the major outcomes for the course. One might also include some of the more subtle, knowledge-based aspects of the course that need to be documented because it has been agreed "students must know this to master the course." Again, it is important to remember that we must 1) agree on what the significant outcomes for the course are, 2) make sure that these outcomes are assessed in meaningful ways, and 3) report these outcomes in the progress report. (It goes without saying that *instruction* is key to the students' success, but that will not be addressed in this chapter.)

This example comes from an actual elementary mathematics document that was written during the summer of 1990. It is not state-of-the-art in format or in content. What educators would now write as course *outcomes* were written more as course *outline topics.* Course topics are listed as follows:

1. mathematics as problem solving
2. mathematics as communication
3. estimation
4. patterns and relationships
5. concepts of whole number operations
6. geometry and spatial sense
7. statistics and probability
8. number sense and numeration
9. whole number computation
10. measurement
11. fractions and decimals
12. mathematical and connections

As noted in the document, most of the goals and objectives have been paraphrased or taken directly from NCTM's *Standards.*

Here is an expanded version of the first outline topic (mathematics as problem solving):

The study of mathematics should emphasize problem solving so that students can:

1. formulate problems from everyday and mathematical situations
2. develop and apply strategies to solve a wide variety of problems
3. use problem-solving approaches to investigate and understand mathematical content
4. justify answers and solution processes
5. acquire confidence in using mathematics meaningfully

How might the third-grade mathematics progress report reflect a student's progress and achievement on these outcomes? First you must close your eyes and imagine that I have, in fact, convened a broad-based committee of stakeholders in this product and that we have agreed on what needs to be reported. Most of what remains involves negotiating on format and fine tuning. (Remember, what I am doing here is not the epitome but rather, the beginning.)

For brevity, the codes to be checked are "N" for not yet, "E" for emerging, and "M" for most of the time.

PROBLEM SOLVING

N	E	M	
			a. formulates problems from everyday and mathematical situations
			b. develops and applies strategies to solve a wide variety of problems
			c. uses problem-solving approaches to investigate and understand mathematics
			d. justifies answers and solution processes
			e. shows confidence in using mathematics meaningfully

Now, where are we going with this? Does this mean we will need a progress report that has, not one or twelve items to check, but perhaps fifty or more? One suggestion is to assess some of the outcomes one reporting period, other outcomes another period, and so on. However, what message does that send to the student and the parents? That problem solving is important the first nine weeks, but not the second? That estimation is not important until near the end of the year?

Clearly, we must modify our reporting methods to include the student's *products*, namely the portfolio. Whether we assign a letter, number, or other mark to the portfolio is probably not as important as being able to see the student's work, having a rubric well in mind so that we know what we are looking for (what is important), and then examining the student's products in the portfolio.

It seems paradoxical to be in a graduate-level education class learning about cooperative learning from a professor who is using the lecture method. It seems paradoxical to be learning about paradigm shifts in assessment and reporting methods in a class that will culminate with a single letter grade (an "A," we hope!) while the readings and the professor point out the shortcomings of this reporting method. What is the solution?

Section Four

MORE TO THINK ABOUT

Chapter 13
Drawing a Portrait of Emergent Learners

KATHY SCHLOTTERBECK

O ver the last forty-plus years, from both sides of the desk, I have seen many forms of evaluation. I know that the manner in which I was evaluated as a student colors my belief about how people ought to be evaluated. In college I was forced to take a tennis class. I started at the bottom of the class, barely able to connect my racket with the ball. Over the semester, I improved in serving, backhand, and forehand volleys. I was able to play a credible game. My friend, a jock of sorts, also took the class. She improved slightly and remained at the top of the class.

My friend got an A and I got a C. I argued that I should also have received an A to reflect the fact that I had improved more. I still got a C. However, this incident caused me to see that letter grades are too narrow to accurately assess learning.

The 1990s have been a period of transition for me, my school district (Topeka Public Schools), and the state (Kansas). I have changed grade level, my school district has changed progress reports, and the state has changed the way it funds school districts.

In 1990, efforts began to make kindergarten classes developmentally appropriate. This meant changing what was reported to parents and ways in which reporting was done. In 1991, a committee of kindergarten teachers and administrators devised a new report card reflecting the philosophical change. The old report card listed discrete skills such as "alphabet," a list of all the capital and lowercase letters with boxes to mark "+" or "−" if the student had mastered or not mastered recognition and/or printing of each letter. Numbers one through twenty-five were listed under "math skills" in the same way as the letters. The letters were listed again under a separate heading, "sounds," identifies/associates. The heading "reading/writing skills" listed these skills: 1) Says alphabet; 2) Hears rhyming words; 3) Puts events in sequence; 4) Prints first name; 5) Prints last name, and 6) Follows left to right progression.

The new report card consists of four separate forms. The first one is information for parents called "Ready or Not . . . Kindergarten Information." This contains the philosophy, some general information, and an explanation of the progress report. There are two reporting forms: a first- and third-quarter review form and a progress report for second and fourth quarters. The review forms are used in conjunction with the parent conferences held during the first and third quarters.

In 1992, another committee began considering a portfolio model for kindergarten through second grade. Checklists of behaviors were devised for speaking, reading, and writing. Listening was evaluated by having the teacher read a story and the student respond to the story. Teachers were to observe these behaviors during the first and third quarters. Only kindergarten teachers continue to use the checklists as of 1993 (see Figures 13–1, 13–2, and 13–3). The new first- and second-grade progress report incorporated many of the behaviors on the list.

The state has mandated that all schools be outcomes based by 1996 to meet the requirements of QPA (Quality Performance Accreditation). This may change our reporting system again. Topeka Public Schools chose three schools to be QPA pilot schools. My school, Randolph, was not in the pilot. As of this writing we have not begun to feel the impact of the change.

In 1991 I moved from second grade to kindergarten. The move was voluntary. Developmentally appropriate practices fit my emerging whole language philosophy. I work very closely with Ann Christiansen, the other kindergarten teacher in my building, who shares a similar philosophy that values individual developmental differences. We seek to measure children against themselves and not to compare one child with another.

We feel that communication with the parents is extremely important. We begin each year with two conferences, an individual and a group conference. In the individual conference we hear the parents' perspective on their child. We ask for strengths, weaknesses, and concerns. Each conference lasts about fifteen minutes.

In the group meeting, we share our view of development by reviewing oral language development and explaining how reading and writing develop in similar ways. We discuss the progress report and how we mark it. We share the checklists written by the district portfolio committee. We discuss our schedule and some of the themes we will pursue during the year.

Kindergarten Portfolio

Speaking

Student: _____

Teacher: _____

(Note to teacher: In the boxes at right, check or date when observed.)

Can Do Checklist

Can Do Checklist	1st	3rd
1. Expresses ideas and shares personal experiences.	✓	✓
2. Responds to reading selections.	✓	✓
3. Participates in recitations such as nursery rhymes, etc.	✓	✓
4. Stays on topic in a group discussion.	✓	✓
5. Formulates questions to get needed information.	✓	✓
6. Adjusts own speech and language to help listener hear and understand the message.	✓	✓
7. Shares her/his written selections with the class and invites discussion.		✓
8. Retells a story.	✓	✓
9. Expresses ideas in an organized manner.	✓	✓
10. Explains and supports personal opinions.		✓

Figure 13–1 *Kindergarten Portfolio: Speaking*

Throughout the year, we send home parent newsletters in which we share ideas, activities, and information about the classroom. To help parents understand why we do what we do, we invite them to participate in the class.

We regularly assess students' progress. We do this through observation during the school day. When a child does something that shows a

Kindergarten Portfolio
Reading

Student: _____

Teacher: _____

(Note to teacher: In the boxes at right, check or date when observed.)

Can Do Checklist

			1st	3rd
Attitude	1.	Listens to stories.	✓	✓
	2.	Talks about stories.	✓	✓
	3.	Chooses to read independently.	✓	✓
	4.	Sees self as reader.		✓
Book Knowledge	5.	*Holds book with print right way up.*	✓	✓
	6.	*Tracks from left to right.*	✓	✓
	7.	*Understands book parts: author; illustrator; and beginning, middle, end.*		✓
	8.	*Understands the difference between fiction and non-fiction.*		
Comprehension	9.	Uses pictures as cues to meaning.	✓	✓
	10.	Makes predictions of story events.	✓	✓
	11.	Predicts repetitive language patterns.	✓	✓
	12.	Retells a story.	✓	✓
	13.	Identifies rhyming words.	✓	✓
	14.	Self corrects when reading.		
	15.	Uses prior knowledge to gain meaning.		
	16.	Uses sounds to decode meaning.		
	17.	Uses context to determine word meaning.		
	18.	Uses word meaning to aid comprehension.		
	19.	Reacts critically to what has been read.		

Figure 13–2 *Kindergarten Portfolio: Reading*

Kindergarten Portfolio
Writing

Student: _____   _____

Teacher: _____   _____

(Note to teacher: In the boxes at right,
check or date when observed.)

Can Do Checklist	1st	3rd
1. Uses drawing for writing.	✓	✓
2. Dictates stories or sentences s/he wants written down.	✓	✓
3. Scribbles for writing.		
4. Uses letter-like forms for writing.		
5. Uses learned letters in random fashion for writing.		
6. Copies letters or words.	✓	
7. Willingly invents spelling for unknown words.		✓
8. Spells some words in conventional form.		
9. Writes from left to right.	✓	✓
10. Uses letters and word spaces meaningfully.		
11. Puts words together in a sentence format.		
12. Talks about what s/he will write.		
13. Uses some upper and lower case letters conventionally.		
14. Uses some punctuation marks conventionally.		
15. Organizes ideas into topics.		
16. Writes on a variety of topics.		
17. Writes across the curriculum.		
18. Uses concepts of order and time in writing.		
19. Shows a willingness to revise and edit.		
20. Chooses and verbally reflects upon favorite writing pieces.		

Figure 13–3 *Kindergarten Portfolio: Writing*

connection, we write it down and often tell the parent that same day. It is at these times that we discover areas that need further explanation to parents. During calendar time, one of my students showed that she connected the pattern between the days on the calendar and the days of music class. I could tell from the mother's reaction that she did not know what I was talking about. I wrote in my notes to talk at length about the important of recognizing patterns in the learning process.

All teachers and parents meet in conference twice a year: the first and third nine weeks. In kindergarten, we send home a progress review form prior to the meeting so that the parents can bring any questions, concerns, or observations to the meeting (see Figures 13–4 and 13–5). We use the portfolios and notes we have taken during the nine weeks to support our assessment.

The second and fourth nine-week progress report uses a checklist format. Ann and I find that this is not enough. We add a narrative to each of these progress reports giving examples of observed performance (see Figure 13–6).

Outcomes for our school and for the kindergarten level have yet to be written. I know they are coming, so I have given some thought to what kindergarten students leaving my class should look like:

- Students feel competent in their ability to learn.
- Students know many stories well enough to enjoy books by themselves.
- Students enjoy unfamiliar stories and have confidence to predict what will happen.
- Students know that what they write is valued by others and have a desire to share it.
- Students value other people's writing and respond in a helpful manner.
- Students are willing to take risks.
- Student are developing the skills that will help them become literate members of our community.
- Student find mathematical concepts meaningful and use them to solve daily problems.

Knowing that change is coming is the only unchanging part of public education. Not all change is good! I believe that it is my responsibility to be open minded but to reflect critically on the changes that come my way. Students benefit in several ways with our current progress report:

KINDERGARTEN

Topeka Public Schools
First Quarter Review

STUDENT _____
PRINCIPAL _____
TEACHER *Schlotterbech*
SCHOOL *Randolph*
DATE *1993-94*

Dear Parents,
   Topeka Public Schools introduces the kindergartener to the school environment by providing a well-balanced program suitable for your child. Kindergarten offers opportunities for the students to explore, discover, and create according to their own abilities and interests. Please look over this review and bring it with you to your scheduled parent/teacher conference. We welcome your questions and concerns.

43 Days Present   *0* Days Absent

Checks (✔) indicate progress demonstrated.

LANGUAGE DEVELOPMENT
✔ shares with group
✔ shares experiences to be written down
✔ learns and shares rhymes and stories
✔ recites personal information

CRITICAL THINKING
✔ understands concepts introduced
✔ identifies shapes and colors
✔ works to develop problem solving strategies
   continues patterns

✔ PARTICIPATES IN PHYSICAL EDUCATION

SOCIAL/EMOTIONAL DEVELOPMENT
✔ follows directions
✔ takes care of personal needs
✔ participates in classroom activities
✔ chooses and follows plans
✔ cooperates in work and play
✔ listens attentively
✔ follows school rules
✔ adapts to new situations

MOTOR DEVELOPMENT
✔ participates in games to enhance large motor skills
✔ demonstrates fine motor development

✔ PARTICIPATES IN MUSIC

TEACHER COMMENTS: _____ has made several friends in the PM class. He enjoys creating adventure stories with the sea creature in the water table, in the block center and in his writing. He knows most letter sounds, but he still prefers to dictate his words for his writing! He can figure out patterns to solve problems.

Original to Parents
Copies to: _____ Teacher
           _____ Student File (record)

Form No. 8413-10 Revised 9/91

Figure 13–4 *First Quarter Progress Review Form*

KINDERGARTEN

Topeka Public Schools
Third Quarter Review

STUDENT _____

PRINCIPAL _____

TEACHER *Schlotterbeck*

SCHOOL *Randolph*

DATE *1993-94*

Dear Parents,
    Topeka Public Schools introduces the kindergartener to the school environment by providing a well-balanced program suitable for your child. Kindergarten offers opportunities for the students to explore, discover, and create according to their own abilities and interests. Please look over this review and bring it with you to your scheduled parent/teacher conference. We welcome your questions and concerns.

42.5 Days Present   *0* Days Absent

Checks (✔) indicate progress demonstrated.

LANGUAGE DEVELOPMENT

✔ shares with group
✔ shares experiences to be written down
✔ learns and shares rhymes and stories
✔ recites personal information

CRITICAL THINKING

✔ understands concepts introduced
✔ identifies shapes and colors
✔ works to develop problem solving strategies
✔ continues patterns

SOCIAL/EMOTIONAL DEVELOPMENT

✔ follows directions
✔ takes care of personal needs
✔ participates in classroom activities
✔ chooses and follows plans
✔ cooperates in work and play
✔ listens attentively
✔ follows school rules
✔ adapts to new situations

MOTOR DEVELOPMENT

✔ participates in games to enhance large motor skills
✔ demonstrates fine motor development

✔ PARTICIPATES IN PHYSICAL EDUCATION   ✔ PARTICIPATES IN MUSIC

TEACHER COMMENTS: ___ does an outstanding job with his writing. He always has an idea which he completes both the illustration and writing before he comes to read it to me. He is beginning to read which he shows when we are reading a big book. He is popular with his peers and treats them with respect.

Original to Parents
Copies to: ____ Teacher
         ____ Student File (record)

Form No. 8413-20 Revised 9/91

Figure 13–5 *Third Quarter Progress Review Form*

SCHOOL YEAR: 1993-94

STUDENT

SCHOOL: Randolph   KINDERGARTEN

TEACHER Schlotterbeck   PRINCIPAL

Checks (√) indicate progress demonstrated.

READING SKILLS

Concept 2nd 4th
Taught QTR QTR

- Understands and remembers story events
- Recognizes rhyming words
- Recognizes beginning sounds
- Demonstrates top, bottom and left, right progression
- Recognizes letters introduced

LANGUAGE SKILLS

- Recites personal information
- Expresses ideas verbally
- Participates in group activities and discussions
- Relates ideas and stories in sequence
- Uses complete sentences
- Listens to gain information
- Creates and communicates in written form

MATH SKILLS

- Understands spatial concepts (over, under, etc.)
- Compares sizes, shapes and numbers
- Uses one to one correspondence
- Sorts and classifies
- Recognizes numerals
- Counts by rote
- Counts with understanding

PHYSICAL EDUCATION

- Participates in activities

MUSIC

- Participates in activities

SOCIAL DEVELOPMENT

Concept 2nd 4th
Taught QTR QTR

- Cooperates in work and play
- Works independently
- Shares with others
- Participates in activities
- Demonstrates self discipline
- Respects authority
- Respects the rights of others
- Follows safety rules

MOTOR DEVELOPMENT

- Demonstrates fine muscle control
- Demonstrates large muscle control

CRITICAL THINKING

- Makes appropriate choices
- Makes independent decisions
- Shows creativity

WORK HABITS

- Follows directions
- Shows effort
- Takes care of materials
- Listens attentively
- Uses time wisely

	Total
Days Absent	0 3 0 6	9
Times Tardy	0 0 0 0	0

Placement for year 1994-95   Grade 1st

Figure 13–6 *Second & Fourth Quarter Progress Review Form*

- The focus is more on what children know than what they don't know.
- It allows a class to have a wide range of successful performance, which begets more success.
- Parents are encouraged to participate in the evaluation process.
- Communication is not limited to four times a year.

Time is the biggest problem with the current form of reporting. Each report card can take from seven to ten minutes to complete. When multiplied by fifty students, that equals six to eight hours of writing time four times a year.

However, the object of reporting is communication. At the present time, face-to-face conferences, supplemented by written narratives, appear to provide the most accurate picture of learning for kindergarten students.

REFERENCES

Smith, F. 1988. *Insult to Intelligence.* Portsmouth, NH: Heinemann.

Chapter 14
Questions Parents Ask

SANDY ADAMS AND KIM YOUNG

A decision to change a reporting system affects many groups, including students, teachers, administrators, school board members, and especially parents. Parents have many questions when change is proposed. This chapter addresses some common questions and concerns. Parents who have actually participated in the change process have contributed questions, explanations, and quotes to help others learn from their journey.

How will my child be motivated without a letter grade?

Many parents are concerned that their child is only motivated by letter grades. William Glasser, in *Quality Schools* (New York: Harper & Row, 1990) says, "In a quality school, there are no bad grades. My guess is that this will be the single most difficult change to make. Teachers, administrators, parents, and politicians will complain that they are being asked to disarm in the middle of a war. Even some students who get good grades may resist. It will take time, patience, and effort to convince teachers to give up the threat of a bad grade, but unless bad grades, with all their potential for coercion, can be totally removed from a school, it will not become a quality school" (106). We need to have ways to motivate students besides the coercion of grades. We should be building self-motivation in children, which is the most powerful kind. Students are motivated by an internal need to progress. By showing and discussing with children their personal progress, we can improve their self-motivation.

> Progress is rewarded. Lack of progress is met with positive solutions, not negative punishment.
>
> Parents of a third grader

Does an alternative reporting system only benefit low achievers by bringing them up to the middle and bringing high achievers down to the middle?

Many parents fear that by not giving letter grades, we intend for all students to attain the same level of learning. However the opposite is true with alternative assessment. In an alternative reporting system, William Glasser also says, "A low grade would be treated as a temporary difficulty, a problem to be solved by the student and teacher working together, with the hope that the student would come to the conclusion that it is worth expending more effort. But besides low grades, any grade, even an A, could be improved at almost any time if the student can demonstrate to the teacher that he or she is now more productive than before" (107).

Letter grades are tied to a percentage. Students who already know the subject will receive high percentages throughout the unit. However, those students who are learning from the unit and do not completely understand the material until the end of the unit will receive a lower grade, because of averaging. They may know the material just as well as the A student at the end of the unit, but they did not understand the material at the beginning of the unit. Many times we evaluate students on something they already know rather than new material.

Letter grades do not encourage students to extend their learning. Students who are given an A are not allowed to continue past the required material for fear of interfering with learning at the next grade level. Teachers should set minimum standards, but not maximum standards. A bright or energetic child should be allowed to go beyond the requirements.

> My daughter usually earns high grades. When I ask her what she needs to improve, she says there must not be anything because her grades are so good. It's difficult to motivate her when I don't know exactly what she should be learning.
>
> Parent of a fourth grader

Should students be using grades to compete with each other in the elementary setting?

- Children must learn to compete.
- We live in a competitive world.

If our students are to become professional athletes, those statements may be true. Most students will enter into a lifestyle (work and social) in which doing one's best and cooperation are keys to success. Yet how many times are adults graded in relation to others in the work place? Fortunately, this does not often happen. How many adult jobs require total self-reliance? Adults work in close association with others. If you are in competition with your fellow worker, this association is strained at best.

The only students who might be motivated to learn in a competitive setting are those who receive A's. These students realize they are learning. They realize they can solve new and difficult problems. They are aware that a recent piece of writing is superior to earlier writings. Teachers communicate to these students about their growth and progress. In other words, students who are doing well are aware of their success. In most cases, these students are intrinsically motivated. External motivation is unnecessary.

Students who receive less than desirable grades are being told they are not measuring up to the other students. These students realize they are having difficulties. The teacher regularly works with them to help them improve. These students do not benefit from being labeled by a grade at the end of the period. They do not need to be reminded that other students are learning more rapidly. Such labels often cause avoidance behavior. Students say, "I can't make the grade in math. I can't do math. I don't like math. I will avoid math."

An alternative reporting system encourages students to compete against themselves. Students' progress is measured against their own abilities.

> The new report card assesses each child's capabilities in a positive and constructive manner. The new method of assessment leaves my children feeling good about the work they have completed each grading period.
>
> Parent of first and third graders

Are letter grades just a number game?

A number or letter grade means nothing without an explanation of the learning involved. Assigning a number or letter in assessment is taking useful information gathered about the student and, by assigning to it an abstract symbol, making it meaningless.

A number or letter grade is often the result of averaging numbers or scores. The final information is, therefore, an average of all the assessments made of the skills involved, and it does not inform anyone about what the student has or has not learned.

People often assume that if an evaluation system does not use numbers, then the system is too subjective to be valid. But if we delve deeper, we find that number systems also are subjective. Some letter grades are based on effort, while other letter grades are based on achievement. In one setting, a less able student might receive an A in math because the teacher felt the student did her best. But in another setting the same A might be based on having made few mistakes on a standard curriculum.

Often, to reach the "magic" number of questions on a test, numbers that factor into one hundred nicely, such as ten, twenty-five, fifty, or one hundred, a teacher might include unrelated questions. Who authored your textbook? Is your name on your paper? Is the correct heading on the paper? These items, which may not relate to the curriculum, are counted as part of the grade.

Scores can be manipulated. Teachers may choose to throw away the lowest score. Maybe the student can earn extra credit points, which will affect the letter grade.

Students are often credited for how quickly they learn. Whenever scores are averaged throughout the grading period, as opposed to determining achievement based on the student's best effort, learning speed is being reinforced. Students are often encouraged to retake a test in hopes of answering more questions correctly. Often a student does not get the opportunity to substitute the second effort's score for the first effort's score; rather, the two scores are averaged together. Again, the measure reflects learning speed and does not give a true picture of the student's achievement.

If *learning* is the message we wish to send to the student and the parent, then educators should speak directly to the objective or desired outcome. Progress toward these outcomes should be rewarded.

> Letter grade systems are not effective in the elementary grades because they do not measure the student's learning or competency, but instead evaluate individual performance based on the total group. Students need to be evaluated on their individual progress in achieving skills, not just in comparison to their peers.
>
> Parent of a fifth grader

What happens after elementary school?

Many parents are concerned about what happens to their child after elementary school. How will the students deal with letter grades in the secondary school and college? First, parents should be made aware that colleges do not look at the child's elementary school grades. Furthermore, secondary schools get a better picture of the student's capabilities looking at a progress report versus letter grades. Many secondary schools receive students from different elementary schools. The students have had many different teachers, who average grades in many different ways. These teachers have used a wide variety of assignments and levels of assignments to arrive at the letter grade. An A for one student may be a B for another because of the difficulty of the assignment and the fact of its having been assigned by different teachers. However, since a progress report specifically outlines objectives and goals for each student, a secondary teacher can clearly see what the student was working on the previous year and can assess the student's ability to perform at a certain level.

Secondary schools are currently experiencing parental and public pressure to accept a nongraded system. Although the practice is not widespread, a few secondary schools and colleges in the United States have already adopted nongraded or portfolio systems for evaluating students' performance.

> The new system more closely mirrors real world situations. Employee evaluations, training progress reports, etc., seldom, if ever, use a grading system similar to the old system.
>
> Parents of fourth and fifth graders

How will the progress report travel from school district to school district?

In our transient society, many families move from one school district to another. Families are concerned about how a different district will interpret an alternative reporting system. An alternative assessment provides a great deal of information about a child, especially if the student is transferring in the middle of a school year. Teachers can see what information students have covered in their previous school and their level of achievement. They can make a broad interpretation and begin students at the point they are ready to begin. Adjustments can be made as needed. However, new students who bring with them report cards with letter grades furnish no information about what they were working on in their previous classroom. Teachers do not know how the grade was earned. Each teacher has different standards. Therefore, most teachers will start at the beginning and make their own evaluation of new students, regardless of the information provided on a traditional report card from the previous school.

> We are able to look beyond letter grades and get a more comprehensive report of the various skills being taught and her progress in learning those skills. We also feel this new report card will assist next year's teacher in sorting out objectives that were not fully mastered, rather than looking at letter grades given for entire subjects.
>
> Parents of a first grader

How can teachers be consistent in their assessment of students?

Inconsistency among teachers of the same grade level can be a problem when using alternative assessment. A percentage scale, which all teachers follow in the letter-grade system is not available. However, how consistent are we when we follow a percentage scale? Many teachers use other factors to arrive at a percentage besides the child's work, such as late papers, tardiness, neatness, discussion in class, and ability. These items are difficult to evaluate in an objective manner or may be irrelevant in demonstrating a child's progress. Individual teachers put different values on outside factors and calculate their effects on percentages differently. Although a number score appears to be consistent, many factors make a percentage grade different from one teacher to the next. A grade of 85 could reflect a student's learning 85 percent of the material, or using 85 percent of his ability, or giving 85 percent of his effort. Unfortunately, a grade of B does not explain exactly what the teacher valued most in determining the grade. Most parents and educators do not have a clear picture of the factors used in determining a grade.

Can we achieve consistency among teachers? Because of differences in teaching styles and assignments, absolute consistency cannot be achieved. Yet a district can move closer to consistency by defining standards and outcomes, and by developing rubrics that will assist teachers in evaluating students. A rubric gives a description of a child at each level for each outcome. A rubric provides a level of standards for attaining each outcome and allows for a comparison of student progress toward these standards. Teachers can use rubrics when discussing a student's evaluation with a parent. The parent knows the entire district is using the same rubric and is therefore holding all students to the same standards, though possibly using a different format.

> I would like to know how my son is doing compared to the other students in his class. Yet, I also want to know how he is doing compared to himself. A single letter grade can't give me all of this information.
>
> Parent of a fifth grader

Should our reporting system be the same for all buildings within our school district?

The school board or parents may be concerned that the report format is not the same throughout the district. Yet the progress report is only as powerful and authentic as the teachers who write it. Therefore, if a committee designs a report card for the district, it will be most valuable for those teachers on the committee. A district committee often includes representatives from a variety of schools with a variety of agendas. Such a diverse group is often forced to make numerous compromises until the progress report is actually representative of no one. These teachers are then called on to go out and "sell" the report to other teachers and their school's community.

However if a site-based council designs a report card for its building, those directly involved in using the progress report will readily see its value. They will be willing to stand behind the report because it was written to meet the particular needs of their building. Every building has a different population with different needs, as outcomes education has shown. Schools can have different outcomes and different goals for meeting the same long-range outcomes, but each building has a different path to follow to reach the desired point.

> Being involved in writing the new progress report helped me understand the changes. Many parents looked to me for an explanation.
>
> Parent of second, fourth, and fifth graders

Why should we change from letter grades to alternatives?

Many people have researched the effects of letter grades on students. David Elkind writes in his book *The Hurried Child,* (New York: Addison Wesley, 1989) "What schools teach children, more than anything else, is that the end result, or grade, is more important than what that grade was supposed to mean in the way of achievement. Children are much more concerned with grades than with what they know. So it isn't surprising that when these young people go out into the work world, they are less concerned with the job than with the pay and the prerequisites of the job. What schools have to realize is that the attitudes they inculcate in young people are carried over into the occupational world" (56).

Educators are emphasizing the grade instead of the student's process and product. They can give children a different message by placing value on the quality of their work. As Glasser explains in *Quality Schools,* "We are not talking about inability; we are talking about not working. We are also looking at a situation that both the students and the teachers in a boss-managed school accept: As time goes on, the A and B students will separate from the C, D, and F students, and by high school they will hardly know each other. As control theory clearly explains, once students get low grades they start to take school out of their quality worlds. They do less work and separate from the students who are working" (105–106). We do not want elementary students to take school out of their "quality worlds." We want to build a good foundation for school to stay in their quality worlds. Glasser continues by saying, "Finally, I ask both the good and the poor students, 'Are the poor students incapable of getting good grades? Are they as a group less capable than the good students?' They assure me that this is rarely the case. They say that if the C and D students worked hard they could do as well as anyone else, and I believe them. We are not talking about inability; we are talking about not working (105).

Using alternative assessment procedures allows students of different ability levels to succeed. They need to see this success to increase the likelihood of success. Experiencing success increases the likelihood of further success.

> It is crucial that our students be assessed in line with the current and future methods of teaching.
>
> Parents of a sixth grader

How do you encourage educators and members of the community to accept an alternative reporting system?

Teachers, administrators, parents, and school board members play an integral part in developing an alternative reporting system. For the project to be successful, each group must be educated about the reasons for changing systems. Teacher in-services, parent newsletters, open houses, and knowledgeable speakers are all ways to educate those involved. An overall plan should be developed that includes the participation of committees at the various stages of development.

Glasser writes, "Before teachers eliminate letter grades in their classes, they should consult parents, explain the reasons for this change, and obtain their agreement to a trial of this approach. If this new way to grade is effective, other teachers will be willing to try. For obvious reasons, in a quality school no attempt would be made by the administration to coerce any teacher into making this change until he or she was ready" (*Quality Schools*, 107).

Many people will find it difficult to change their thinking about letter grades. For several years, these grades have been an integral part of our educational system. Some people will not give up letter grades without a struggle. These people will need many concrete examples of the harmful effects of letter grades on our children.

> I was invited to a gathering at the home of our principal to discuss the progress report. This informal setting helped me feel comfortable enough to express my concerns and ask questions.
>
> Parent of a second grader

It is imperative to address parents' concerns and questions if the community is to accept a different reporting system. A climate of openness must exist between home and school so that parents feel comfortable expressing themselves, and show a willingness to discuss new ideas. Such a climate often takes time to develop, but the investment is well worth the time.

Chapter 15
Student Self-Assessment
ELIZABETH SCHMAR

I wont to Be abl tuwrite longr
Stres, and Read Bedr.

During the first week of school, Danny, a third grader, wrote this goal for the upcoming school year. Danny's goal, honest and to the point, really puts our purpose for being at school into perspective. Along with addressing the goals of the school curriculum, we must also respond to the goals of our students.

My role as Danny's teacher is to create a classroom environment filled with activities to help Danny and other students reach their goals. Throughout the year, I will teach Danny to evaluate his progress toward that goal using his own standards. Danny's evaluation could be as informal as a teacher-made questionnaire or as formal as an attachment to the progress report completed by the student.

Our goal as educators is to help students become self-evaluators, not only in their school work, but in their everyday life. We, along with their parents, will help students establish inner standards they can use to determine quality. We guide them in helping themselves answer the question "How can I tell if my work is really good?"

As teachers, we constantly ask ourselves, "Am I doing a good job as a teacher?" As our teaching experience increases, we develop an inner yardstick to measure our classroom successes. Some questions we may ask ourselves are:

- Do my students appear enthusiastic and seem to enjoy the things we do in class?
- Am I able to make ideas from one subject area tie into another so that students make connections?
- Am I prepared with materials appropriate for the developmental needs of my students?

We then compare our answers to these questions with our inner standards of what determines a quality teacher. Our success at teaching is determined by information we gather from students, parents, administrators, and ourselves. We somehow fit those opinions into our own schema of what makes a good teacher to determine our level of success, and set our goals from that point.

In some situations, outside standards are imposed to determine our success as teachers. A person outside the classroom might use standardized test scores, letter grades, or even the noise level of our classroom to determine the quality of our teaching. We might feel the need to make changes or "improvements" in our teaching to fulfill some outside requirement. But working toward our own personal high standards will make more lasting and higher-quality improvements in teaching.

Students can evaluate themselves in the same way teachers evaluate themselves. Once students have established their inner standards and have those anchored firmly in place, they can determine their own level of success. Our outside standards of letter grades and test scores continue to keep students from fully developing those standards. We are continually placing students in a situation in which we, as adults, are determining their standards of quality. So students spend their time trying to meet our standards rather than putting effort into developing their own. We are fostering dependent evaluators when what we should value are independent evaluators. To change this pattern, we must provide students with time to look at themselves through their own eyes. This searching helps both the teacher and the student learn about progress made during the school year.

INTERNALIZATION

Student self-evaluation is a way for teachers to know whether students have internalized their learning. We often wonder if concepts students learn will be retained long past the time they leave our classroom. By writing thoughts about their learning, students are forced to use metacognition, or thinking about their thinking. We talk with students about the process of learning, setting goals, and essential practice. We want to help them develop a view of themselves as a learner by looking at their strengths and weaknesses. We emphasize the process of learning rather than just the final product. Children experience this value of process every day during writing workshop. They can easily see that becoming a good writer requires a goal toward which to work, time, and practice.

Students are now looking at their learning on a different level than just memorizing facts, completing a work sheet, or taking a test. Their learning becomes an integral part of the self.

Jessica writes,

Well, its different than my first story, because it tells about more importain things than just a story. It shows that I improved sence 5th grade. This paper shows I learned better use of words, I like my style of writing better now. than before.

Teachers feel a sense of satisfaction when children realize the value of learning.

Jill writes,

I like learning because I know it'll help me later in my life. One behavior I have is that I know that if I mess up, it's not the end of the world.

The best way to know whether students develop a love of learning is to ask them to tell us. We won't find out from a test score, a letter grade, or even a traditional report card.

HONESTY

Once we give students opportunities to evaluate themselves, we will begin to see a sense of honesty develop. For many students, initial self-reflection is very superficial. They may be testing the waters to determine the teacher's *real* motivation. Or they may never have been given the opportunity to view themselves in a reflective way. Once the initial wariness passes, a refreshing honesty can be found in student responses. A rapport may develop that is seen in no other aspect of the relationship between student and teacher. This feeling of openness encourages students to take a long, hard look at themselves. The view in the mirror is not always pleasant even though it may be true. Koty saw a true picture of himself when he evaluated his science project on the digestive system:

"I could have put more in and used more class time and not goof of as much."

As teachers, we may have made this type of comment to a student like Koty, but when he makes the comment to himself, change is more likely to occur.

When asked to evaluate a piece of his own writing, Luke writes:

If you trie to reach a goal
it may seem hard at first
But if you work tords
that goal and practice,
you will acomplish it,

As adults, we try to instill this value in children by our words and actions. When a student reiterates this thought independently, it is a gratifying event for a teacher and a meaningful one for a student.

GATHERING INFORMATION

Developing a sense of honesty between student and teacher takes time and practice. How much depends on the openness and readiness of the student, together with the modeling and atmosphere created by the teacher. The time taken to build rapport is extremely well spent because the teacher can gain vast amounts of information about the student as a learner. Koty writes:

> My weekness is probably Science. I'm not very good at it. It's harder to understand.

Science may very well be hard for Koty to understand, but it also is possible the science book is above Koty's reading level. He may need extra help or more time to read his assignments. Courtney writes:

> I'm not real good at answering questions unless I can get them strait out of a book or notes.

Reading comprehension seems to be difficult for Courtney. I could teach her strategies to help remember details from reading.

Lee's goal for this year is to "think of better iddas for writing." So during a writing conference with Lee, I will focus on techniques for generating ideas, such as brainstorming, noticing ordinary events, and borrowing from other people.

While the students are viewing themselves as learners, we as teachers are also gathering valuable information. We can use these insights to make instructional decisions for individuals, small groups, and the whole class. Our newly gathered information also adds another dimension to our view of our students and how to best help each of them.

The benefits of developing self-evaluators are many, both for the teacher and student. But honest self-reflectors are not created overnight. As with anything worthwhile, a commitment of time and patience is necessary.

Some key strategies will help make the process go more smoothly for everyone involved:

- Model self-assessment.
- Develop an atmosphere of acceptance.
- Provide a variety of opportunities for practice.
- Design the tool to seek the information you desire.
- Value student reflection as much as other forms of evaluation.

Model Self-Assessment

From experience we learn that actions speak louder than words. In the case of self-reflection, this concept is especially true. It is not enough for us to just tell our students to evaluate themselves; we must demonstrate we value self-reflection by reflecting on ourselves.

During the first few weeks of school, I always use the example with students of my inability to draw on the chalkboard. Our conversation might go like this: "I am not good at drawing, but I will try my best to draw for you, as long as you promise not to laugh. Now this is supposed to be a map of the United States."

A few giggles come from the room, and someone says, "That looks like a buffalo!"

I say, "I know, I told you I wasn't very good. Maybe if I erase part of this line, and move this up. Well it's still not great. I could use the overhead projector or make a big map on tagboard to trace around."

Already I am modeling for the children that I am aware of my weaknesses, yet I am willing to try my best. When my best attempt is not so good, I think of ways to compensate for my weakness by using a projector or tracing. The students need to hear me think aloud so that they follow my thoughts and hear appropriate comments.

When I first begin using goal-setting activities with the class, I describe the goal-setting process teachers go through with their principal. I may even go so far as to tell the students one of my professional goals for the school year. For example, one year I focused on developing my skills at using the computer. Once my students knew my goal, whenever they saw me working on the computer, they knew I was working on my goal.

I also describe for them the teacher self-assessment checklist our district uses to help us work toward becoming better teachers. The checklist is broken down into six main categories with five to thirteen activities in each group. I will even read the list to myself and complete it while the students complete their own self-assessment form. I am modeling the physical act of reflection—sitting quietly thinking, writing, then thinking and writing more.

We usually write one simple personal goal every few weeks on a self-assessment form for daily work, to be sent home with students for the parent's signature. In writing my goal, I try to select something that can easily demonstrate progress to myself and the students. The goal of keeping the top of my desk clean is usually where I begin. I try to make sure the desk looks messy to begin with so we all can see lots of progress. Some students select the same goal I model, which can be an indication they are not yet ready to take the risk of looking closely at themselves. Others might choose the goal of neater handwriting, a good performance on a test, or not getting into trouble. Students who are willing may share their goals, which give others ideas for future goals. Some students even tape a copy of the goal to their desk as a constant reminder.

During the next week or two, I ask students how I am doing on my goal. Then I give them a few minutes to reflect on their own progress. Willing students can share about the struggles and successes of working toward their goal. In this way, their reflection is serving as a model for others.

At a predetermined time, individuals decide if their goal has been reached. Then the students may write a new goal or continue on the same path. Twice a year the parents become involved in writing goals with the student. At a parent-teacher conference, evaluating progress and writing new goals becomes the central focus (see Figure 15–1).

Once the students have been through the goal-setting process several times, they will begin to set their own goals as needed, without prompting by the teacher.

I want the students to realize that growing as a learner and a teacher involves a continual process of goal setting, practicing, and evaluating progress. My participation in the process has a great impact on the value they place on the process.

Develop an Atmosphere of Acceptance

From the first day of school, the classroom atmosphere must be one of acceptance of all students regardless of their developmental level. This atmosphere is created by accepting all attempts to open up and share through writing, speaking, and making choices. Students must feel their risk taking will be positively received by other students and the teacher.

One of the best ways to encourage risk taking is to put myself in a vulnerable position by taking a risk and using reactions by other students as models. Although some aspects are similar to the modeling concept, this time I focus on the attitude of acceptance students display toward me.

While teaching a mini-lesson during writing workshop, I display an overhead transparency of my story with purposeful grammatical and

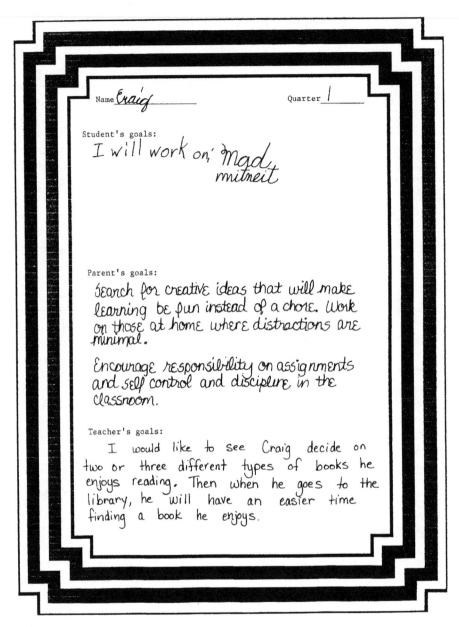

Figure 15–1 *Collaborative Goal Sheet*

organizational errors. Although the obvious intent of the lesson is to develop editing skills, I am actually putting my writing and ultimately myself on the line. While making changes suggested by the students, I focus on the appropriateness of their comments, tone of their voices, and their use of nonverbal cues. Students can observe my response to criticism and their classmates' attempts to critique my writing without hurting my feelings. Following the lesson, we discuss the positives and negatives of the classroom situation.

The school day must be filled with sharing activities for the atmosphere of acceptance to really develop. Students will develop acceptance and risk taking at different rates. We must acknowledge even the slightest effort and reward that effort with recognition.

Provide a Variety of Opportunities for Practice

As with learning any new skill, practice is the key to developing quality self-reflection. Most students will write something on the paper when asked, but that's as far as many will go—just something on the paper. We are actually seeking in-depth inner reflection. The skill of reflection does not come naturally to all students. Fortunately, there are a few who will pour their hearts out with little or no prompting. We get a wealth of detailed information from even their first attempts. For others, unfortunately, writing even one personal comment is either a slow, laborious task or a quick, superficial one. The range of risk taking is a true reflection of the range of abilities and personalities in a classroom.

Teachers should expect students to develop quality responses at different rates. Given this expectation, we must provide ample opportunities for students to practice self-reflection.

Judging the quality of one's work can be integrated into any subject area. A "reflection activity" can occur at the end of a thematic unit, upon completion of a project, or at the end of a designated time period. The reflection time should be a natural part of the classroom activities.

The most necessary component of self-reflection is thinking and writing. Therefore, students must be allowed time for these. This time must be uninterrupted by noise, distractions, and other assignments. There must be an ample amount of time, because reflective thoughts may not come easily for some students.

By our providing a productive atmosphere, students learn we value their ability to collect their thoughts about themselves and put those thoughts on paper.

Design the Self-Reflection Tool to Seek the Desired Information

When designing a self-reflection program, teachers should first formulate their purpose. For me, that purpose is twofold. I am looking to gather information regarding my students and their development. I also want my students to notice their progress and write a quality reflection. I define a quality reflection as a display of in-depth and honest comments about one's work and progress. To bring about such a reflection, I formulate instruments that encourage students to write in this way (see Figure 15–2).

Here are some guidelines for developing effective instruments:

- Write open-ended questions, making it obvious there is no one correct answer.
- Provide ample space between questions to encourage students to write several complete thoughts.
- Design questions that focus students on their strengths, weaknesses, and goals.
- Consider using a continuum, which often helps students who are visual learners.
- As the teacher, verbally express the value of in-depth and honest responses. Some students feel more comfortable sharing if they know the teacher is the only one reading their paper.

Developing effective instruments takes practice. Like the students, teachers are developing new skills in this area. Initial instruments may not generate the desired results. But this situation will improve as the teacher's purpose becomes clearer and students practice self-reflection skills.

Value Student Reflection as Much as Other Forms of Evaluation

Student self-reflection is a piece of the total evaluation picture when looking at the whole child. In the past, we have tended to value those pieces of information to which we could attach a number or score. Numbers appear easy to interpret for teachers, parents, and the general public. The supposed objectivity of numbers has actually misled people into believing in their superiority as an evaluation tool. Recently we have come to realize that numbers give us little, if any, useful information for organizing our classroom and planning instruction.

We gain valuable information from observing, anecdotal records, conferencing, reading logs, journals, taping, and student self-assessment. Each of these assessment tools is one piece to help us put together a total picture of the child.

Name Tyson   Date 10-27-93

WRITING EVALUATION

	Weak	Good	Excellent
Ideas			
topic is appropriate for school	____	____	__X__

B^+

Organization			
story makes sense – could be longer	____	__X__	____
Conventions			
uses accurate spelling	____	____	__X__
uses correct periods	____	____	__X__
uses correct capital letters	____	____	__X__
Publishing			
book reflects much effort	____	____	__X__
neatness used in writing	____	____	__X__

Teacher comments:

You are right, the story is not long enough. You have an excellent beginning of a story. You have told me enough to make me want to read more. The typing is nicely done!

STUDENT EVALUATION

What are the best parts of my story?

The tiping
The tidle

What part of my story would I like to improve for the next time?

not long enohg.

Figure 15–2 *Writing Evaluation*

My Personal
Report Card

What are your strengths? Write about school activities you are good at or enjoy doing.

I enjoy social studes and Geography

What are your weaknesses? Write about things you are not good at or would like to improve. I really don't think I have a real weakness. But I would like to improve in health.

What kind of attitude do I have about learning? Write about your behaviors in school that help you learn or keep you from learning. I think I have a good attitude about learning. When I don't have work. I kind off hang-out. But when theres work I try to be serious.

What suggestions do you have to make this school year good?

I don't have any suggestions. (Can't think of any)

Figure 15–3 *My Personal Report Card*

A quarterly reporting system is commonly used for sharing information with students and parents. Self-reflection activities should be included in this reporting system because they are just as important as the information reported on a progress report (see Figure 15–3). Written reflections can be shared at a conference or as an attachment to the more formal progress report.

I have my students use their portfolio as a basis for their reflection. Their portfolio is a collection of work over time. The students select one of their best pieces of work to evaluate. Their selection is made based on their own definition of quality work. Occasionally their selection is not the piece I would have chosen. But for self-evaluation, students must be entrusted to make their own determination of quality. I may select a different quality piece for another type of evaluation. The portfolio and evaluation are shared with parents at conference time or photocopied and attached to the report card to be sent home with the student.

Students and parents learn our classroom values by seeing the time and effort we put into a project. If we stress the importance of self-reflection as an evaluation tool, they will pick up on our cues and also develop this value.

Chapter 16
Expanding Reporting Options Through Technology

MIKE KASNIC

O ver the years, the central focus of the instructional management process has been the teacher. The teacher's major role has been to provide the appropriate educational program for each student. As technology becomes an important aspect of this process, the teacher's role has been greatly expanded. If the teacher is to enhance the productivity and management of the classroom, technology can become an important tool in the process. Pencil, chalk, and eraser have been tools for the teacher over the past century. Technology is a tool that affords the teacher unlimited opportunities to monitor and respond to individual student needs.

Technology will significantly change the way student achievement is reported both to parents and to official student records. As schools and teachers move toward authentic or alternative assessment, technology will become a vital component in the collection of student data. The major questions to be answered are: how much data should be collected regarding the knowledge individual students possess, in what manner should it be stored, and how should it be reported. This chapter describes some of the ways technology can help schools address these important questions.

ASSESSING BOTH PROCESS AND PRODUCT

Educators continue to debate the proper mix of assessments. In the meantime, technology companies, colleges and universities, and individuals are busy working to provide teachers with new tools for assessing their students. These tools can be divided into three major categories: electronic portfolios, observational tools, and scoring systems.

ELECTRONIC PORTFOLIOS

The field of educational technology is evolving on an almost daily basis. New techniques, hardware, and software continue to be developed and implemented throughout education. With that in mind, what follows is a description of four initiatives currently underway in the use of electronic portfolios.

The first initiative is the Coalition of Essential Schools, which is working with IBM's EduQuest division to pilot "The Digital Portfolio." Mickey Revenaugh (1993), in *America's Agenda*, describes it as:

> a computer-based system for collecting and analyzing "exhibitions"—the student products and performances that Coalition schools require as demonstration of mastery. Using LinkWay hypermedia software, the program records objectives which can then be matched against scanned-in essays, video clips of oral presentations, and other materials. (32–34)

This exciting joint venture with digital portfolios is further described by David Niguidula (1993) in "The Digital Portfolio: A Richer Picture of Student Performance":

> The Digital Portfolio is a computer-based tool for what the Exhibitions Project of the Coalition has termed "planning backwards." A school can approach decisions about its system of education by addressing a series of three questions:
>
> 1. What should a graduate of this school know and be able to do? The answer to this question is the "vision" of the qualities that a graduate—any graduate—should possess. The vision needs to be created by the school community, led by the faculty that will be looking for those qualities in their classrooms.
> 2. How can a student demonstrate the skills and knowledge that a graduate should have? In other words, how would we know that a student has the qualities to fulfill our vision? Here, the answer might take the form of a set of "exhibitions" or other performance-based assessments completed either individually or collaboratively.

3. How can the school arrange its systems so that all students can exhibit the desired skills and knowledge? This is where the real work of school change begins. The school needs to look at all its systems—curriculum, pedagogy, assessment, scheduling, administration, and so on—in an honest attempt to determine if the decisions it makes are helping students fulfill the vision. Often this takes a great deal of "rewiring" of communication within the school—not just with physical wires, but by creating a structure of time and space that allows everyone involved with the school to communicate.

> The Digital Portfolio represents a tool that may help a school develop some preliminary answers to these questions. We can imagine many possibilities for the use of digital portfolios, but as often happens with technology, imagination runs far ahead of reality. Our primary goal, however, is not technological; rather it is to devise a tool that can help schools develop a richer picture of what students are capable of doing. (12)

The second initiative in the area of electronic portfolios is being developed by Scholastic Inc. This company has developed a portfolio tool that lets teachers explore students' work over time. This software was originally designed as a multimedia tool in the area of social studies. Revenaugh (1993) states that:

> Evolution of the software as a portfolio tool began when two Vermont teachers adapted the company's "Point of View" multimedia timeline to store students' artwork, writing, video clips and sound bites in chronological sequence. The portfolio product allows teachers to explore all of a student's first-grade work or all of her science projects and grades 1–6; they can even download a series of samples of videotape for the students to take home to Mom and Dad. (34)

A third initiative in the area of electronic portfolios is the Grady Profile, developed by Emily L. Grady. Aurbach and Associates, Inc. (1993) describes the Grady Profile in a brochure:

> The Grady Profile is an electronic portfolio that records achievement—without turning a student Portfolio Assessment into a statistic. The Profile follows students' work and behavior over their school careers. It replaces an annual score on a permanent transcript with a fair portrait of a growing person. Using The Grady Profile is like having all the files on a student open at one time. You can assess a student completely, efficiently and multi-dimensionally with one tool. Assessing students with the Grady Profile helps you integrate evaluation into your curriculum and turn assessment into a proactive agent for learning. (1)

The brochure lists the following capabilities and features:

- Record basic information found in a Central Office file including a photo
- Quickly assesses academic and social skills using behavioral descriptors. The teacher, student and family can all participate in the assessment process.
- Record observations and anecdotal remarks about student performance

- Record a student reading aloud, speaking, playing an instrument
- Scan student writing, math problems, art or other graphical images
- Individualize the Profile to meet each student's needs by changing objectives, adding custom cards and renaming cards to meet your goals
- Keep all of a student's data in one place
- Store QuickTime movies of kids in action
- Note standardized test results
- Maintain strict confidentiality—authorized users see only the records they need
- Print anything in the Profile for one student or all students

The fourth initiative in the area of electronic portfolios is called AIMS, or Abacus Instructional Management System. AIMS is probably the most comprehensive curriculum development and instructional management system available in education today. It is included in this section on electronic portfolios because AIMS now has the capability to drop into IBM's Linkway software so that electronic portfolios can be developed. AIMS is described as follows:

> AIMS is an instructional management system that is designed to assist the teacher in the management of instruction on a continuous basis. The benefits of AIMS are directed to the teacher, and indirectly, to the student. It provides insights that come from having broad, current information about mastery of instructional objectives in a class, school, or district. The system assists the teacher with organizing the curriculum, test generation, scoring tests, locating instructional resources keyed to objectives, and offers diagnostic information about student achievement. By relieving the teacher of burdensome clerical tasks, it saves time that can be spent in planning and working with students. (Abacus Educational Systems 1993, 6)

"AIMS allows teachers to easily provide:

- continuous monitoring of individual student progress
- diagnostic placement of ability grouping
- increased individual attention
- detailed reports for conferences
- immediate feedback of test results with diagnostic information
- comprehensive library of learning resources
- individualized education plans" (6)

OBSERVATION TOOLS

Many assessment experts support student evaluation that is "embedded" in the learning process: teachers observe children as they work on projects or problems and record observed levels of mastery. Teachers who have attempted to take and use anecdotal notes during the teaching and learning process know how much time and effort it takes to go through the process with paper and pencil. Technology that supports this process includes the Learner Profile and the personal digital assistant (PDA).

The Learner Profile is a hand-held system developed by Sunburst/Wings for Learning. The teacher uses a credit card-size optical reader and a list of personally created observational criteria that have been translated into bar codes. As a teacher circulates around the classroom, student behaviors are scanned from a set of bar codes corresponding to proficiency levels the teacher has developed. This scanning can be performed anywhere, including the classroom, gymnasium, laboratory, out-of-doors, and on field trips. At the end of the day, observations that have been stored in the card-size scanner can be electronically transferred to a Macintosh computer.

The process works as follows:

1. At a Macintosh computer, student names, the observational criteria to be used, and any additional qualifiers are entered. A printout gives all of the names and criteria in bar code form.
2. While working with students throughout the day, the teacher simply scans the student name, the behavior observed, and the appropriate qualifier with the scanner. The scanner allows up to two thousand observations a day.
3. At the end of the day, the teacher inserts the scanner into a small uploader to transfer the observations into the computer, making it possible to generate class and individual reports for review.

Teachers who have worked with the Learner Profile and bar code scanner report that they can record their observation immediately, can determine beforehand the specific behaviors they want to look for, and can make observations on an ongoing basis. The Learner Profile also allows the teacher to work with students individually to set specific goals for that child. In using the scanner, the teacher remains within the learning process, pausing just a moment to scan the child's name, the behavior, and any appropriate descriptor.

An assessment device such as the Learner Profile can help schools look at student development over time rather than simply looking at an end product.

Personal digital assistants are hand-held, electronic message pads, about the size of a paperback book. Operated with a stylus, they have the capability to interpret the recorder's handwriting. Writing is done directly on the LCD panel and converted to text. This text can then be downloaded into a

Macintosh or MS-DOS computer for use in a word processor. PDAs have potential future applications as observation gatherers, allowing teachers to record, organize, and analyze their notes on student learning.

PDA technology is still in the infant stage. New systems are being developed daily. If development continues, use of a PDA by every teacher, not only for recording student observations but for every other aspect of teacher use, is not unrealistic.

SCORING SYSTEMS

Large testing companies are beginning to enter the portfolio and alternative assessment area. National Computer Systems, Inc. (NCS) sees a role for new technologies in portfolio management. Isabelle Bruder (1993) quotes NCS vice president Robert Bowan:

> We are adding electronic imaging to our instructional management system. With electronic imaging, teachers can build portfolios by capturing student work in various formats, be it handwritten, computer-generated, video or audio. NCS has plans to use the imaging system in national programs, such as NAEP (National Assessment of Educational Progress) tests, to help store everything from written essays to traditional bubble test answers. (27)

Mickey Revenaugh (1993) says NCS is exploring additional areas of assessment.

> Testing companies such as National Computer Systems, Inc. (NCS) are exploring technological aids to efficiency and effectiveness in the scoring of open-ended tests. The NCS imaging system, for example, lets scorers evaluate essays and solutions on-screen, using computer tools, while the system adjusts for human quirks that can throw reliability off. (34)

The Defense Department, in conjunction with the Educational Testing Service, has developed computerized standardized tests that adjust to the ability level of the test taker. As the test taker proceeds through the test, artificial intelligence adjusts the level of the test down if too many incorrect responses are made and up if the test taker is giving many correct responses.

But the most exciting use of technology in test taking might occur in the very near future. Educational Testing Service and the Defense Department are working on multimedia and multisensory simulations of a very complex nature. Students are challenged to solve complex, open-ended questions, and technology is used to keep track of the logic students use in solving the problems.

Perhaps Revenaugh (1993) sums up the situation best:

When it comes to testing, technology plays it both ways. It's a driving force behind standardization, behind those multiple-guess bubble sheets and the electronic scanners that spit out percentiles and mean scores. But the advocates of authentic assessment with their portfolios, performance, and open-ended prompts can also claim technology as their ally. They're engaged in a struggle to redefine the nature of the tool, from efficiency-master to creative assistant. (32)

The technology of alternative assessment is as dynamic and ever-changing as every other area of educational technology. What is new and exciting today will be outdated in six months.

REFERENCES

Bruder, Isabelle. 1993. "Alternative Assessment: Putting Technology to the Test." *Electronic Learning* (January):22–29.

Niguidula, David. 1993. "The Digital Portfolio: A Richer Picture of Student Performance." Studies on Exhibitions (No. 13), Coalition of Essential Schools, Brown University. Providence, RI.

Revenaugh, Mickey. 1993. "Machine-Gauged." *America's Agenda* (Fall):32–34.

1993. *The Grady Profile Can!* Brochure, Aurbach and Associates, Inc. St. Louis, MO.

1993. "ABACUS: Instructional Management Systems." Booklet, Abacus Educational Systems. Portland, OR.

Chapter 17
Shifting Paradigms

TARA AZWELL AND GORDON GULSETH

The idea for this book burst into my mind one morning in 1991 as I was watching a video, "The Business of Paradigm." In the video, futurist Joel Barker discussed the changes in perspective that human beings must be willing to make to successfully face the future. He stated that the mindset lens through which we view the information available to us virtually determines what we see. Our paradigms can prevent us from seeing alternative ways of solving our problems.

Barker challenged viewers to ask a most important question about their fields of endeavor: "What is impossible to do, but if it could be done, would fundamentally change your business?" As I listened, I heard the voices of teachers, administrators, students, and parents commenting to me repeatedly, "But if I do that, how will I grade it? I must have a grade for the report card." Reasons that there "had to be a grade" were numerous. Parents expected letter grades. Students wouldn't do the work unless it was graded. Students must have grades to be admitted to college and to receive scholarships. Grades are needed to determine members of the honor roll.

Because a letter grade was needed for the report card, teachers believed that they must collect data that could be averaged for a final grade. Some districts went so far as to require a certain number of homework grades, a certain number of class activity grades, and a certain number of test grades each reporting period. Standard ranges of percentages were designated for each letter grade. Such procedures were mandated by the central administration to ensure uniformity of grading throughout the district, to be certain that teachers were fair and, most importantly, to discourage teachers from slacking off in their duty to demand rigorous work from their students. Grade books were regularly collected and examined to verify that the required entries were indeed present.

In American schools, we too often tend to employ the mindset lens of ancient academics in examining information. According to Evans Clenchy (1994), American schools are "decontextualized" from everyday life. He argues that examinations are part of a "scholastic sorting and elimination process that does its best to fix every child's place in later life . . " (747). Furthermore, he states that "The Great American Academic and Social Sorting Factory School System must be recontextualized so that what students learn and the way that they learn it is reconnected to the larger society" (747).

Clenchy blames the emphasis on "standardized paper-and-pencil tests of academic skill and/or letter or numeric high school grades in conventional subjects" for allowing institutions of higher education to keep all of our lower schools in thrall to their disconnected decontextualized educational mission (747).

The preceding chapters highlight the problems of current reporting systems. They also provide examples of ways some teachers and school districts are attempting to better communicate information about what has been learned to students, parents, and other teachers. In the effort to restructure schools to improve their ability to support students as they learn, four factors should guide our thinking:

1. The focus of all our attention must be student learning.
2. For students to become lifelong learners, they must become self-referenced learners.
3. Teachers are professionals who have the knowledge and skills to help students learn.
4. Students, parents, and teachers must communicate and collaborate to help students learn.

A FOCUS ON STUDENT LEARNING

Many schools have adopted mission statements asserting, "All students can learn." This is a lofty statement. What is needed is that our practices become congruent with our words. Benjamin Levin (1994) argues that students are not the raw material, not the workers, and not even the product of the school in the same sense that the terms *raw materials, workers* and *products* are used in industry. He states, "Education is a unique kind of production, because it requires learners to create knowledge and meaning in the context of their own lives . . . . literature suggests that the most effective strategies have to do with treating students as capable persons, capitalizing on their knowledge and interests, and involving them in determining goals and methods of learning" (759).

Such an argument would also support the necessity for students to be involved in the assessment and evaluation of their own learning. Portfolio assessment and student-led conferences are a step in this direction.

Levin goes on to suggest that students are "persons who need to be autonomous in a collegial setting, who need to exercise more influence over their work, who should not be arbitrarily assigned work or evaluated without their participation" (760).

The need for students to be partners in planning and assessing their own learning has become very clear to us as educators. We realize that because knowledge is increasing at such a rapid rate, we can no longer predict what information and what skills students will need when they complete their formal schooling. Gordon Gulseth has served as an elementary school building principal in Kansas and Wisconsin. In grappling with curriculum development and assessment and reporting systems for his schools, he came to realize that for students to truly become lifelong learners, they must become self-referenced learners. He shared the following thoughts on this important concept.

STUDENTS AS SELF-REFERENCED LEARNERS

What is it we hope to achieve with all of the varied and numerous forms of student assessment? Certainly in some minds the thinking is that assessment will directly or indirectly promote a certain level of proficiency or mastery by the teacher and/or the student. Some would maintain that assessment is "data collecting" and should be used to chart progress. Still others would maintain that assessment and learning are two sides of the same coin, and that the eventual goal is to promote lifelong learning by helping students understand how to use a variety of assessment techniques so that they may chart their own progress and develop the ability to "self-assess."

The "standards" approach ensures that large groups of students will have similar knowledge and skills. The question of who determines the standards, and for what age, readily comes to mind along with other concerns, such as whether or not this approach promotes a simplistic view of learning that does not encourage higher-level thinking. Collecting data on student performance could provide some information, but in all likelihood this data would have a numerical format, and there are limits as to what information can be relayed through numbers.

If the goal is to encourage lifelong learning, it would seem that continuous self-assessment is not only desirable but necessary. In fact, it seems ridiculous to even consider that adults would use norm- or criterion-referenced tests to determine their intellectual growth. In some rare cases, such as the written portion of vehicular driving tests, it may be one of the methods used but certainly not the only one. Instead we rely on feedback from colleagues, family, and friends, and most importantly, on insight gained from previous experiences. In fact, referring to our previous performances and experiences may be the most reliable way to chart our own growth.

The concept of self-reference may already exist in many schools. Portfolios, when students are allowed to determine content, include this self-referral element. Self-evaluation forms, if designed by the student, would also encourage self-referral.

Authentic assessment approaches may or may not promote this concept. If the work is authentic only to the school environment, then it is someone else who has determined what has value or "worth." While it is important for students to know what other people value, the goal is to help students become confident in their own ability to make value judgments about previous and future actions, and using this information, to chart a course that is not only self-determined but self-enhancing.

In contrast to self-referenced assessment, most of the current approaches that are used to judge an individual could be called "other referenced." They have a tendency to promote extreme competition between and among individuals. These approaches compare the student to external standards. They include the "ideal student," "situational assessment," and "object-based" assessment. The "ideal student" approach (outcome based, standards, etc.) is very prevalent and needs no comment. "Situational assessment" refers to a special activity such as a sport, or even a certain aspect of a sport. "Object-based" assessment refers to the concept of defining who we are by what we own. The popular bumper sticker "He who dies with the most toys wins" readily comes to mind, and although it is meant to be humorous, it certainly has a dark side. An "object-based" approach to judging someone would not play the same role in school that it does later in life; however, it is obvious that this becomes important very early as evidenced by stories of students who are shot for their jackets.

As can be imagined, a constant comparison to external standards could lead a student to have difficulty deciding with what or whom to identify. If one's identity is always defined externally, the question of "self" tends to lose significance. Instead of developing and recognizing individual uniqueness, the student begins to relate to objects and/or groups. Independent thinking is replaced by the latest fad, fashion, or advertisement, or by the desires and inclinations of the group.

The alternative is to help students become self-referenced in such a way that external factors are always considered but are secondary to the growing awareness of "self." These external factors can then be judged by the individual in terms of how they will affect the self, and a determination made as to their value. Granted, positive and negative role models play an essential role in this emerging sense of self, but as independence grows, the self-referring individual develops the ability to constantly refer back to previous experience and to the status of the self to determine personal orientation to things, people, and situations.

This brief discourse attempts to apply a personal philosophy of growth to the challenging and somewhat confusing world of educational assessment. While the ideas discussed are somewhat abstract, "nature abhors a vacuum," and time will provide the opportunity to either fill in the gaps with more concrete ideas or replace them with other ideas more worthy of consideration.

TEACHERS ARE KNOWLEDGEABLE PROFESSIONALS

Through our attempts to develop and use "teacher-proof" material and strategies, we have come to a startling realization. Learning is a very people-dependent process. Learning, growing, and changing usually occur as a result of interactions with others. Most learning takes place through contact with people who are more knowledgeable than us about what we are trying to learn. Brian Cambourne (1988) identifies conditions that foster learning: immersion, demonstration, expectation, responsibility, approximation, employment, and feedback. Teachers have been trained to establish the conditions needed to foster learning.

Most teachers care deeply that their students learn. Teachers spend many hours with students while they are involved in learning. They have many opportunities to observe and interact with students as they learn. And teacher judgment about student learning has been found to be as reliable as (and perhaps more reliable than) many more formal evaluation procedures. In a meeting of people working with a state board of education to develop a state reading test, the director of a prestigious testing center stated that if the opinions of the classroom teacher about the status of a student's learning differed from the information provided by "his" standardized test, he would defer to the teacher's judgment. These were startling words to those attending. However, almost every teacher can recall times when standardized tests painted pictures of students that they did not recognize. Yet even though teachers knew their students very well, they were often not allowed to use their professional judgment to select appropriate instructional and assessment strategies. Teachers are told that to ensure "rigor," a certain number of students should fail. They are told what kind of evidence they can consider to determine the extent to which learning has occurred. They are told what kinds of information they must share with students, parents, and other teachers, and in what format it must be.

Barr Raebeck (1994) suggests that schools must become more people centered. He states that too often our schools, which are charged with helping students to succeed, "argue against higher rates of achievement and express satisfaction with significant levels of failure among workers" in an effort to insure quality and rigor (762).

STUDENT, PARENT, TEACHER COLLABORATION

An old African proverb states, "It takes the whole village to raise a child." What an accurate statement! Yet in our society, we have fragmented those efforts. Parents support this, churches support that, and on and on. To make matters worse, often the different parties fail to accept their assigned roles or are unwilling to abdicate a certain role to another party.

Learning occurs best when it is intentional—when what is to be learned is clearly defined and indicators of success have been identified. These can best be identified through communication and collaboration. Student-parent-teacher conferences are one way to begin. So are portfolios, in which students, parents, and teachers all have input about what will be collected.

As my undergraduate class was discussing these issues, one student exclaimed, "But you are talking about an IEP (Individual Education Plan) for *every* student!"

In truth, I am. Each student is unique; each has a unique learning style, a unique set of background experiences, a unique set of goals and interests. Learning is a very personalized thing.

Yet most students share a common set of things to be learned and are capable of cooperating and collaborating with others even when pursuing different ends. Teachers who encourage student decision making and student responsibility in the learning community have been dealing successfully with individual learning plans for years. Their major problem has come when they were forced to report the status of each student's learning in a standard format that often attempted to compare one student with another.

Through collaboration and communication among all interested parties, better ways to provide information about what a student knows and has done can be developed.

REFLECTIONS

In the first chapter of this book, we invited you to join us on a journey to explore ways to address concerns about report cards and reporting systems. This leg of the journey has ended. However, the journey is not over. We have just begun to explore the possibilities. New, better ways to provide accurate feedback to learners about the state of their learning are yet to be discovered. We invite you to continue the journey and share your discoveries with us.

REFERENCES

Barker, Jim. 1990. "The Business of Paradigms." Burnsville, MN: Charter House International.

Cambourne, B. 1988. *The Whole Story: Natural Learning and the Acquisition of Literacy in the Classroom.* Auckland, NZ: Ashton Scholastic.

Clenchy, E. 1994. "The Albatross Around the Neck of Our Public Schools." *Phi Delta Kappan* 75 (10):745–751.

Levin, B. 1994. "Improving Educational Productivity: Putting Students at the Center." *Phi Delta Kappan* 75 (10):758–760.

Raebeck, B. 1994. "The School as a Human Business: Organizing Problems Out; Designing Productivity In." *Phi Delta Kappan* 75 (10):761–765.